BALANCING ACTS

Essays on the Teaching of Writing
In Honor of
William F. Irmscher

EDITED BY

Virginia A. Chappell
Mary Louise Buley-Meissner
Chris Anderson

Generously Donated to

The Frederick Douglass Institute

By Professor Jesse Moore

Fall 2000

Southern Illinois University Press ▲ Carbondale and Edwardsville

Copyright © 1991 by the Board of Trustees,
  Southern Illinois University
All rights reserved
Printed in the United States of America
Edited by Dan Gunter
Designed by Kristy Robinson
Production supervised by Natalia Nadraga

Library of Congress Cataloging-in-Publication Data

Balancing acts: essays on the teaching of writing in honor of William
  F. Irmscher / edited by Virginia A. Chappell, Mary Louise Buley-
  Meissner, Chris Anderson.
      p.   cm.
    Includes bibliographical references.
    1. English language—Rhetoric—Study and teaching.   2. Irmscher,
  William F.   I. Irmscher, William F.   II. Chappell, Virginia A.
  III. Buley-Meissner, Mary Louise.   IV. Anderson, Chris, 1955–
  PE1404.B25   1991
  808'.042'07—dc20   90-36155
  ISBN 0-8093-1638-2   CIP
  ISBN 0-8093-1639-0 (pbk.)

Frontispiece: William F. Irmscher

The paper used in this publication meets the minimum requirements of
American National Standard for Information Sciences—Permanence of
Paper for Printed Library Materials, ANSI Z39.48–1984. ⊚

Contents

*I*ntroduction

Balancing Acts celebrates the contributions of William F. Irmscher to the field of composition studies as a whole and to the individual professional growth of many composition scholars and teachers.

This festscrift began as a conversation among its three editors at the 1988 meeting of the Conference on College Composition and Communication in St. Louis. We wanted to dramatize the debt that many of us beginning our careers owe to Bill's generous guidance, and we wanted Bill to see that the profession as a whole recognizes that it, too, owes a great deal to him. Before the coffee cups were ready for refills we knew what we would put together: a collection of essays about the teaching of writing—the focus of Bill's own work and scholarship for over thirty years.

We started by planning a panel for the 1989 CCCC in Seattle, an appropriate place to honor Bill since he directed the composition program at the University of Washington there for over twenty years. We asked Bill himself to chair the session and in the meantime, without his knowledge, began soliciting manuscripts for a book.

The metaphor of "balancing acts" presented itself as soon as we started corresponding about the collection. We wanted to acknowledge the breadth of Bill's interests and the practicality of his analysis. Terms such as "pragmatism" and "common sense" kept coming up. As an editor and leader within CCCC and the National Council of Teachers of English, Bill has promoted the work and careers of a wide range of scholars. As a mentor Bill has never represented a single school of thought, never attempted to mold students in his own image, but instead has encouraged his students to pursue their own interests and speak in their own voices.

Still more important to us than Bill's scope and inclusiveness has been his ability to synthesize, to find the center. As former students we each remembered moments when he had curbed excess, counseled compromise and limits, showed us ways of blending and merging what seemed to be conflicting points of view. Bill was always open to new ideas, but he also worked to reconcile those ideas with the practical: the day-to-day demands of student writers struggling to express themselves and the perplexities of young composition teachers struggling to teach new writers. He was a theorist, one of the first to bring theoretical respectability to composition studies. Yet whatever the complexity, however high the stakes, Bill always strove to express the issues in clear and fluid language.

For him, we realized, it was all a question of finding balance: among theories, between theory and practice. "Balancing acts" seemed to capture that Irmscherian spirit, while at the same time acknowledging the precariousness that the three of us, at least, feel as we cross the threshold into a new composition class. The balance to be maintained is our own, as we walk what often seems a tightrope within the composition classroom and within English departments. And it is something that we must establish among myriad responsibilities and allegiances—which we sometimes feel called upon to juggle like so many spinning plates and painted balls—as we help our students develop as writers.

"Balancing acts" is a metaphor that acknowledges complexity and difficulty. Yet it focuses attention on a center. A center and an edge. It echoes Wayne Booth's image of the rhetorical stance, a concept we and countless others met first through Irmscher's *Holt Guide*. It's a metaphor affirming Kenneth Burke's conviction that language should serve as "a symbolic means of inducing cooperation," that as rhetoricians we should seek "identification" rather than difference.

This leads to a final layer of the metaphor. The issue for us as editors of this book is not just honoring the past but reminding the profession of some essential values. Composition studies seems to us just now especially prone to excesses and imbalances. There is an understandable but dangerous drive toward what could be a tyrannizing theoretical order. In the face of such intensity, we asked our contributors to help us honor Irmscher with a calling back to the center: to the concreteness of the teaching moment itself, to the concreteness of the everyday—however complex the theories that describe that concreteness.

The two sections of this collection suggest two ways to describe and organize key issues in the profession. Part 1, "Identity and Community," presents essays about helping students explore both their identities as writers and the effectiveness of those identities within communities of writers. Part 2, "Intuition and Institution," focuses on the dynamics of teachers' decision making about theory and pedagogy within their own institutional communities. The resonance between these two general sets of concerns—the students' and the teachers' (which always include the students')—invokes again the doubled balancing act of the juggler on the high wire.

Kurt Spellmeyer opens the collection with "Balancing Ax: Efficiency and Struggle in English 101," an essay that challenges us to teach writing as a process of exploring differences and establishing commonalities among members of a society divided economically, linguistically, and politically. In his view, the aim of rhetoric should be not more efficient communication, but "a society more open to unfamiliar voices." Similarly, in "The Description of an Embarrassment: When Students Write about Religion," Chris Anderson reminds us that "academic language is not the only language" used by our students to express the truths that they live by. What Chris asks us to value—in our teaching as well as in our students' writing—is critical reflection on the beliefs that shape our sense of reality and possibility. Then, in "Rhetorics of the Self," Mary Louise Buley-Meissner takes up this call for affirming diverse student voices and questions contemporary literary theory's dismissal of an autonomous *I*. She presents careful readings of student papers that reveal the act of writing to be inevitably an act of "self-representation," an attempt "to shape the words and thoughts giving rise to our consciousness of who we are." Against the ground of these assertions of student writers' authority, the next two essays assume a more social view of composing, nevertheless insisting that we respect the fragility and power of students' developing voices. Reviewing current discussions of the ways and means of teacher response to student papers, Virginia Chappell advocates "Teaching like a Reader Instead of Reading like a Teacher," a pedagogy grounded in transactional reading theory and epistemic rhetorical theory. In "Talking about Writing and Writing about Talking," Kathleen Doty, a linguist, shows how insights and methods from the field of pragmatics can apply in the writing classroom as a way of enabling students to discover the power and diversity of language as social, meaning-making activity. Offering us the insights of a master teacher, Edward P. J. Corbett concludes the first section with "Mutual Friends: What Teachers Can Learn from Students and What Students Can Learn from Teachers." As the rhetorician must realize the signal importance of audience, teachers, he says, inevitably learn that in the end they are defined by their students.

Christine Farris leads off the second section of the book with "Critical Reflection, Change, and the Practice of a Theory of Composition," a detailed examination of how new graduate student teachers make decisions in their classrooms. The ethnographic methods of her research, she argues, suggest methods for critical reflection upon evolving theory and practice and so can be adapted for use in the training of new teachers. The value of self-reflection also informs "Practicing Theory/Theorizing Practice" by Anne Ruggles Gere, who highlights the importance of the teacher-researcher in redefining our understanding of "professionalism" in composition studies. She suggests that the most effective teacher-researcher is one who recognizes language's power in "creating culture rather than isolating the truth," a power that inextricably links composition studies and cultural studies. Richard Lloyd-Jones then ventures to describe "A Balanced Survey Course in Writing," one that engages students in discovering language's capacity to name, question, and sometimes change fundamental social relationships. Language, he tells us, is "a designed map of an aspect of reality"—and as our understanding of the map changes, so too does our awareness of the terrain we are crossing. Next, Richard Young cautions us that writing-across-the-curriculum (WAC) programs cannot provide an all-purpose map suitable for every discipline. In "Designing for Change," he recommends evolution—"continuing, adaptive change"—as the model for WAC design. He emphasizes the necessity of dealing with "the new and unanticipatable" while at the same time working out of a consistent theoretical framework. In the book's closing essay, "Teaching as an Act of Unknowing," Charles Schuster also asks us to consider what we might gain by focusing on change rather than stability, particularly the kind of change in perspective exemplified by Bakhtinian concepts of the threshold, novel, and dialogism. He says that in composition classrooms where students are challenged to think and speak and write as individuals (indeed, in the classrooms that all the contributors to *Balancing Acts* are trying to create), "ultimately what is learned far exceeds what is taught."

The volume's final selection provides a bibliography of the work of our honoree. Richard Tracey's title, "He Takes the Teaching of Writing Seriously," sums up the common sense, unpretentiousness, and care that we have learned from the man and his work. This book is a call to remember, as Bill Irmscher always has, that at the heart of this whole enterprise are the student writers themselves and the complexity, the opaqueness, the humanness of the act of composing.

Collaborating as editors has been a real balancing act, too—an Irmscherian enterprise. We have listened and learned from each other; there is little in the shaping of this volume that originated with one of us and not the other two. We have given ourselves permission to say what we really think, as Bill has always done with us. Delineating the places where we overlap and agree, we have worked to "identify" with each other, in Burke's sense of that word. In a small way, then, our collaboration is also a way of acting out what Bill has taught us.

However, even the sublimities of collaboration could not enable the three of us to put this book together without outside help. We extend special thanks to Regina R. Bergner of Marquette, not only for her unfailing good spirits as she compiled the lists of Works Cited, but also for having the good sense to suggest that she be our research assistant in the first place. We are grateful for the support of the departments of English at our three universities—Marquette, Oregon State, and the University of Wisconsin–Milwaukee—and to Professor James E. Swearingen and the Marquette University Graduate School for making possible Ms. Bergner's assistantship. We acknowledge, too, the efforts, encouragement, and enthusiasm of colleagues who are not officially represented here by texts. Finally, we thank Kenney Withers of Southern Illinois University Press for sponsoring this project and for helping us spring the surprise on Bill at our 1989 CCCC panel in Seattle, where Kenney stretched publishers' protocol and handed out announcements of *Balancing Acts* to a large audience of friends, supporters, and former students. We hope that the book that has evolved since, and unfolds before you here, offers a few more surprises and a great many conversations.

Part I
Identity and Community

1

*B*alancing Ax: Efficiency and Struggle in English 101

Kurt Spellmeyer

Peace is something we must *fight* for.
—Kenneth Burke

Every institution might be said to perpetuate its authority by means of a collective forgetfulness. The institution I wish to discuss is freshman English; the forgetfulness is our denial of the violence we routinely inflict upon students. We have forgotten that the history of English 101 begins with an effort to overcome, through the enforcement of a putatively common language, the absence of other, more fundamental commonalities—cultural, political, economic. We have forgotten too that such enforcement did not become socially imperative until after the first half of the nineteenth century, when the small, select number of Americans attending college still spoke in the measured voice of a single class, an agrarian aristocracy on the British model (Rudolph 54–98). We should remember, as well, that even while education of a later day, education at the service of the modern industrial state, could not afford to be exclusive in quite this same way, the need for a work force both literate *and* disciplined required that literacy itself should be used as an instrument of exclusion—if no longer the exclusion of people, then the debarring of alternative forms of speech and thought. In the name of science, the new curriculum promoted the regimen of the factory; and in the name of tradition, it valorized the smooth, complaisant language of the salesroom. Either as fact or as revealing fiction, this account of our institutional past may help us to undertake a task we can neglect only at the cost of continued violence: the task of reseeing our present assumptions and practices, which have not brought us closer to the ideal of a common language but still compel us to maintain the illusion of its attainment.

Recollecting the Past

Although teachers of writing often imagine themselves to be the heirs of classical or eighteenth-century rhetoric, the birthplace of freshman English was actually the new American university in the early decades of our own century—"new" by comparison to the smaller, less diversified colleges that preceded them. The specific need for something called "composition" arose in response to the changes attendant upon large-scale industrialization: the decline of the traditional humanities curriculum, the proliferation of specialized disciplines, and the opening of higher education to populations never before enfranchised. While Harvard College established the first composition requirement in 1874, freshman English as we know it appeared almost half a century later in the vocational and "democratic" university of the Progressive Era (Berlin, *Rhetoric and Reality* 20; Veysey 57–120). The charge of the new university, with courses in accounting, journalism, dentistry, and commerce, was no longer the reproduction of culturally foundational values, but the training of a class of upwardly mobile specialists.

Fittingly enough, then, the predominant motif in the discourse on composition, roughly from 1910 until the end of World War II, was the need for "efficient" language, a language standardized in vocabulary and diction, of course, but also in the practices of textual construction. As Burges Johnson and Helene Hartley announced in their 1934 publication *Written Composition in American Colleges,* "Business and Society find these young American college graduates inadequately trained as writers" (virtually the same complaint made by E. D. Hirsch, Jr., several years ago).[1] To ascertain the extent of the crisis, they interviewed "bankers, insurance presidents, manufacturers, engineers, the heads of great business enterprises," who unanimously ratified the blunt judgment of Frank Presbrey, an advertising agent quoted at some length in the first chapter:

My experience is that nine out of ten college graduates
are wholly deficient in even writing a good letter. When
I say good I mean a letter which is well constructed,
presents the thought or opinion of the writer in a clear,
concise way, with a sequence aimed to create a favorable
decision in the mind of the recipient. (7)

It would scarcely be an exaggeration to claim that Presbrey's notion
of "good" writing has defined for composition teachers ever since an
absolute horizon, beyond which they must not lift their eyes. No
textbook, to my knowledge, has ever honored complexity over con-
ciseness, truthfulness over a "favorable decision," the indeterminacy
of questioning over the tidiness of closure. But I would submit that
the valorization of clear, concise, and ingratiating language does
violence to language itself as an expression of social life, a life which
is, if I may belabor what ought to be obvious, multifaceted, highly
mutable, and fraught with contradiction. Precisely because we inhabit
a world whose dividedness our words makes explicit—in the manner
of our speech, in what we say, and in what we seek from the act of
saying it—the goal of linguistic consolidation, so appealing to Johnson and Hartley's entrepreneurs, could be pursued along only two
possible lines: either by allowing a dialogue that frankly acknowledged diversity as its starting point, or else by waging a protracted
war against diversity of every kind. Tough-minded as Presbrey may
have seemed in his time, nothing could be more airily abstract than the
notion of a language without difference, without dialogue, without
struggle.

But struggle was exactly what our forerunners tried to elude by
means of a precarious bargain. On the one hand, the ostensibly
democratic expansion of higher learning undertaken at the start of
the Progressive Era has been genuinely successful, delivering to mil-
lions of Americans the upward mobility it promised. On the other
hand, it has advanced a narrow range of social interests in a fashion
that is anything but democratic. Broad-based mobility was achieved
at the cost of an unprecedented normalization of public life and,
consequently, the growing estrangement of private life from it: today
speech in the public domain entails a scrupulous silence on matters
private, an active "forgetting" of those forms of experience and reflection least amenable to what Raymond E. Callahan describes as the
"cult of efficiency." In the NCTE monograph *The Teaching of College
English,* for example, Oscar James Campbell, a contemporary of John-

son and Hartley, espoused what has since become an article of faith
in our field: "Language is an essential part of the process of thinking.
It is not the medium, but the means of thought; not its garment, but
its incarnation. Inaccurate, ambiguous, and hazy language is thought
of identical quality" (7). From this moment on, speech at variance
with the spirit of efficiency becomes a *symptom* that calls for therapeutic intervention and a restructuring of subjectivity itself: not simply
untruth (as deviant speech would have been for the Greeks or the
Scholastic philosophers), it gives evidence of a cognitive deficiency.

So thoroughly did the twofold phenomenon of normalization
and estrangement shape the professional common sense of writing
teachers that the social and historical dimension has all but disap-
peared from our understanding of language, as if thought really could
be the same for every age, every class, and every occasion. However
we may think "in our heads," and however we may speak among
ourselves, the reification of "clear thinking" actually served to conceal
the disjunction between life and work, experience and formal knowledge, by presuming the universal applicability of a particular dialect
of English at a particular moment in the history of the language—a
particular dialect, and beyond this, specific and highly circumscribed
modes of reasoning. Yet Campbell himself admits what his successors
have continually rediscovered: "Efforts to define at all precisely what
mastery of usage a freshman should show have not been entirely
successful" (21). While no one is actively opposed to clear writing
(except perhaps the French), neither can anyone identify its precise
characteristics to the satisfaction of everyone else, even within a single
discipline. If one writer's "clarity" can elicit from another the charge
of imprecision, then perhaps the term denotes something besides a
state of mind or a moral condition, something closer to the reassur-
ance we feel in the presence of people who share our values and social
interests. But who shares them all the time? Not only does the
conflation of good writing with clear thinking "forget" the vital
relationship between language and context, between my words and
their meaning in my world, but it forgets as well the embarrassment
of our sociocultural riches—the persistence of different worlds, and
the value of difference itself. This forgetting, however, was an important function of the freshman English apparatus, which otherwise
could never have credibly advanced a particular tradition of writing
and thinking as everybody's "real language" in the face of ubiquitous
evidence to the contrary.

Hence the police component of writing instruction, perhaps the element our students remember most often despite *their* collective forgetfulness. One early Progressive Era handbook opens, for instance, by affirming that the

> first and most important quality of good English is unity. Unity requires that a composition should give the impression of dealing with only one subject, that a paragraph should give the impression of dealing with only one branch of the subject, and that a sentence should give the impression of dealing with only one thought. (Edgar 3)

Obviously, real-world writing often violates these tenets. I am just now recalling the "impression," far afield of unity but somehow deeply meaningful, left by Emerson's famous paragraph in "Experience," the one beginning, "Illusion, Temperament, Succession, Surface, Surprise, Reality, Subjectiveness,—these are threads on the loom of time, these are the lords of life. I dare not assume to give their order, but I name them as I find them in my way" (272). What the author of the handbook voices, however, in still another *locus classicus* of the field, is the institutional resolve to define a standard of mass production, a standard which has only the most tenuous relationship to the history of English prose as written by those who came before Emerson, and by those who have come after: Bacon and Browne, Lamb and Coleridge, Ruskin and Pater, Alice Walker and Clifford Geertz. Strictly speaking, the English of freshman English was not found, but manufactured between the years of 1910 and 1940. Like the Tudor tract house in Arizona or the Thanksgiving Day celebration of "our" Pilgrim heritage, this ersatz, pared-down English simplifies and monumentalizes history in order to escape the reproach of its true complexity.

Although the authors of the early books on composition often refer to their texts as rhetorics, they ignore the fundamentally dialogical character of rhetoric in the classical tradition they claim to recall. For Aristotle, rhetoric was primarily concerned with the political praxis of a society—with the resolution of differences between competing groups by appeal to common values and the shared desire for a good life (1.2–5).[2] Persuasion as Aristotle conceives it does not advance the interests of one group at the expense of the others, nor is it an art of salesmanship employed to curry favor with the powerful. Persuasion begins with the effort to identify commonalities *already existing* between divergent factions, commonalities to serve as the foundation for uncoerced dialogue. And dialogue establishes the

frame of reference for administrative, legal, and ceremonial activities
expressing a true con-sensus or like-mindedness. Far from attempting
to mandate an ahistorical, acontextual definition of clear thinking or
persuasive speech, Aristotle considers a diversity of interests within
the *polis* to be an inevitable part of its ongoing life, and he therefore
affirms the need to determine the available means of persuasion "in
any given case." While persuasion aims at the attainment of mutual
understanding by appeal to those values which seem "self-evidently
true," the self-evident is never self-evident to begin with. Rather,
it becomes evident through the open-ended process of collective
deliberation. On these terms, however, the "rhetoric" of efficiency
operates as an antirhetoric, quietly prohibiting deliberation while
loudly proclaiming uniformity—loudly enough, at any rate, to prevent the emergence of any genuine con-sensus.

No less than the *ekklesia*, or assembly, of Aristotle's day, the classroom is a point of intersection between dissimilar social groups, each
with its own "language," interests, and values. The values of the
home and the neighborhood, for example, seldom correspond to the
assumptions informing disciplines like history or anthropology. By
the same token, the "local knowledge" of black students who grew
up on the broken sidewalks of Newark differs in many important
respects from the worldview of white teenagers raised beside the
backyard pools of suburban Montclair. To diversities of this kind the
antirhetoricians of the Progressive Era responded with a genial *fiat
lux,* bestowing upon everyone the privilege of speech, in theory. In
practice, however, their seemingly egalitarian gesture concealed a
structural contradiction between the classroom as a social space,
the public forum for a conceptually enlarging conversation, and the
classroom as an instrument of socialization, the scene of an initiatory
ordeal. Caught between the two horns of our institutional dilemma,
student writers found themselves in the paralyzing situation of having
to speak while suffering punishment for what they said and how they
said it—punishment for the violation of rules which often seemed
trivial, arbitrary, and even irrational. (Many of us can still recall one
prominent feature of almost every textbook published until quite
recently, an elaborate table of rules/offenses like the one reproduced
in figure 1–1, usually found inside the front cover and resembling
the periodic table of chemical elements with its numbers and occult
notations.) The rationality of our "public" discourse in English 101
was predicated, then, upon an irrational separation of learning from
social life, of Language from the student's own language, and of

THE MANUAL

(The numeral names the page on which the subject begins)

GRAMMAR	Nouns 181	Pronouns 182	Adjectives 184	Adverbs 185	Verbs 186	Conjugation 188
	Voice 191	Infinitives 191	Participles 192	Verbal Nouns 192	*Shall* and *Will* 193	Prepositions 198
	Conjunctions 201	Interjections 203	Phrases 203	Clauses 204	Sentences 206	Definitions 209
SPELLING	Sound 174	*IE* and *EI* 175	Reductions 176	*C* and *G* 177	Stressed Vowels 178	Prefixes and Suffixes 179
PRONUN-CIATION	Obscure Vowels 163	French Sounds 163	*F* to *V* 164	Early Stress 164	Late Stress 164	Stress and Meaning 165
	Silent Letters 165	Vowel Shift 168	"Long" *U* 168	Palatal *I* 170	*Varia* 171	Influence on Spelling 174
PUNCTU-ATION	Comma	Importance 88	Series 91	Dependent Clauses 93	Causal Clauses 94	Coordinate Clauses 95
		Relatives 96	Parenthesis 98	Ellipsis 101	Comma Sent'nce 101	With Other Marks 103
	Semicolon 104	Colon 105	Period 108	Exclamation 109	Interrogation 109	
	Hyphen 111	Syllabication 111	Compounding 113	Apostrophe 116	Quoting 117	
	Quotation Marks 118	Italics 120	Parentheses 121	Brackets 122	Dash 122	
WORDS	Present 4	National 5	Reputable 7	Synonyms 7	Too Few 12	Too Many 13
	Glossary 18	Simplicity 27	Figurative 29	Threadbare 34	Trite Quotations 36	General Exercise 59
SENTENC-ES	Loose 37	Periodic 38	Unity 40	Coherent Connect'n 44	Coherent Arrangem'nt 45	Coherent Structure 47
	Paralleling 47	Point of View 49	Subordination 52	*Which* and *This* 54	Emphasis 57	General Exercise 59
PARA-GRAPHS	Loose 65	Semi-Periodic 66	Periodic 68	Prefatory 68	Transitional 69	
	Developing 71	Summarizing 71	Unity 73	Coherence 74	Emphasis 77	
LARGER UNITS	Outlining 79	Unity 83	Coherence 83	Emphasis 84	Revision 84	
	Titles 86	Explanatory Writing 233	Critical Writing 313	Biographical Writing 351	Persuasive Writing 381	
	Pictorial Writing 411	Narrative Writing 458	Letter-Writing 560	Familiar Essays 585	Translating 614	
TECHNI-CALITIES	Manuscript 125	Note-Taking 129	Composition Noteb'k 130	Borrowing 132	Speaking 134	Oral Reading 139
	Capitals 219	Numbers 220	Abbreviations 221	Notes on Reading 157	Books for Writers 158	Written Exams 140
READING LIST	Biography 145	Essays 148	Fiction 150	Poetry 154	Drama 155	The Bible 156

Figure 1–1. H. Robinson Shipherd, *Manual and Models for College Composition* (Boston: Ginn, 1928). Table of rules/offenses with page references, printed on the inside front cover.

Reason from the student's own reasons: that is, from her personal motives and the values of her community. The cost of empowerment in the classroom was, by this measure, a corresponding disempowerment. Students were granted the privilege of speech, provided they said what their teachers expected to hear.

Reseeing the Present

But teachers of composition also paid a price for their "solution" to the "problem" of cultural and linguistic diversity. I have often thought that "A Modest Proposal" and "Shooting an Elephant" appear in so many anthologies because Swift and Orwell, powerless witnesses to the destructive contradictions of colonialism, mirror our own bad conscience at having to extract from students a single kind of speech while demanding so wide a variety of silences. One recently published textbook/reader which has helped to discredit the unitary ideal responsible for our divided loyalties is *What Makes Writing Good: A Multiperspective,* edited by William E. Coles, Jr., and James Vopat. This text, composed of extended commentaries by distinguished teachers on the essays of their students, openly acknowledges a diversity in both the linguistic worlds of our society and in the criteria that teachers apply to the work they evaluate. It seems to me, however, that one entry, the paper and comments submitted by William Irmscher, goes the editors one better by challenging many beliefs, long axiomatic, about the nature of good writing and the need for a standardized language. Whereas other contributors to the collection discussed the work of students who were exemplary writers by conventional standards, Irmscher selected a paper many teachers would dismiss as severely deficient. The paper, by Shawn McGinnis, was a response to the question, "When is the last time you made an important choice about your way of life?":

> I made an Important decition on finding out what happen when I die. DEATH its a word that makes the strong and rich men tremble with fear. Why would I choose such a subject like death when people try to run from it. Its only becouse I've seen death stalking old people. Playing hide and go seek with young men on the battle feilds. Its also becouse death has no mercy on its choosen victims. Children my brother my grandmother her faveriote pet a

> good freind. They come into my life than leave with
> deaths touch. I've seen death but I never felt it, the cold
> touch of death. forever I will be looking over my shoulder
> for death. I will never really know what its about intel
> that last minute that last breath it might happen next week
> or in fifty years. It will change my life dramaticly, yes. For
> now I'll only think about it. (17–18)

Rereading this brief essay after more than four years, I am once again impressed by its rhetorical power, a power all the more impressive considering the difficulty of the subject. As Nancy Sommers observed in a talk at the 1988 CCCC, among the hundreds of essays she read for the Bedford Prizes competition, none elicited responses more predictable and less meaningful—less successful in representing the experience of the writer—than those dealing with the subject of death. But the force of Shawn's paper derives precisely from its success as a representation, an attempt to evoke the conditions of his life by employing the idiom of ours. Except for the perfunctory opening line, which he abandons along with a question that must have seemed no less perfunctory to him, every word is the product of deliberate choice. When I first came across Shawn's essay during the final stages of a dissertation on self-construction in the seventeenth century, I was struck by the similarities to John Donne's *Devotions upon Emergent Occasions,* with its inconsistent spellings and erratic punctuation—with its offenses, in other words, against basic tenets of "good writing" today.

I do not mean to imply that Shawn is another John Donne (who cares about that?), but it might be worth asking why most teachers would never approach his work with the hermeneutic openness we readily bring to "real" writers of the past. In reading Donne we discount—no, we are fascinated by—those deviations from our current usage which reflect his particular social and historical situation, since we believe that he speaks not just as one person who happened to elope with Anne More and then suffer a series of career reversals, ending his life a celebrated Anglican preacher; we hear him also as the voice of a "period" and a "tradition," and we might reasonably expend five or ten years in the attempt to create an interpretive framework which, rather than suppressing the differences, would make them the object of serious reflection. But Shawn too speaks for something more than himself. Like Donne, he opens to view a world different from ours in its language, its history, its material conditions.

For many teachers, this insight—that "our" society contains a diversity of worlds not encompassed by familiar proprieties, about which people distinctly unlike us *will* speak in a language more or less dissimilar to ours—is so disconcerting that they might prefer to read student writing unburdened with any real content, since a standard product, no matter how inane, at least permits them the illusion that their values really are universal.

If Shawn does indeed speak for something more than himself, *we* speak for something less than Reason or the English language. The qualities we often associate with good writing are not transhistorical, transcultural universals, nor are they even endorsed with any degree of consistency by "experts." And this is just the point that Irmscher makes in his commentary on Shawn's text. Many "of our differences of opinion about excellence among experienced writers revolve," as he contends, "around stylistic differences and matters of taste. Some readers like parallel structures; others do not. Some like loosely connected, associative prose; others do not." Granting this diversity, we "should differentiate . . . between what we like and what we recognize as good writing" (19). If I read Irmscher correctly, he equates "good writing" with hermeneutic sophistication: he praises Shawn's essay for its proficiency as a symbolic action which consciously mediates between the street, where people die by violence, and the academy, where this violence has meaning only as an object of aesthetic contemplation or sociological analysis. In Irmscher's own words, Shawn "wanted to write" and he "had something to say"; he chose a tone, a diction, and a "voice" or persona appropriate to his audience as well as to his particular situation.

With the predictable objections in mind, Irmscher then provides an edited version of Shawn's preliminary draft, deleting the first sentence and correcting the mechanical errors. Although I will not reproduce the edited version here, if skeptics reading my remarks on Irmscher's remarks make the necessary corrections, they will probably accept his conclusion, just as I do: "in terms of content, structure, diction and style, this brief passage represents qualities of good writing" (20). As long as we strain to hear our words in Shawn's speech exactly as we would say them, he will certainly remain a "deficient" writer. But when we become attentive to the interanimation of languages his essay brings about, we can appreciate the extent of his success in the struggle to occupy a linguistic and cultural middle ground. Shawn appropriates the language of the academy so fully that it has ceased to impose a silence on the world from which he came—a silence familiar to many "better" students—enabling him instead to cross over from that world into ours. Weighed against this achievement, the problems with punctuation seem relatively trivial, a question of "mechanics" in the root sense of the word, as a "contrivance," a (merely) strategic aid to communication, and Irmscher says as much at the close of his commentary.

Imagining the Future

But from some teachers, nevertheless, Shawn's essay might receive a very different reading, one that presupposes his basic incapacity. By exposing the violence inherent in such a reading, a violence directed not only against Shawn but also against Shawn's language and the social world which created it, Irmscher puts into practice the theory of communication implied by Kenneth Burke's motto, *Ad bellum purificandum,* "towards the purification of war" (*Grammar of Motives* untitled first page, also 442). So thoroughly has the ethic of efficiency dominated our thinking about language that it may now seem absurd, even perverse, to associate dialogue with the discord of war, yet this is where Burke and Irmscher each begin. Communication, as Burke recalls for us in *A Rhetoric of Motives,* is a response to *dis*agreement, a symbolic action that seeks to mediate between different social scripts, different "orders of motives" (11). Although miscarriages of communication may occur through deductive or inductive error, deduction and induction themselves both rest upon an invisible foundation of basic premises, and it is here, on the level of what Burke variously terms "identification," "placement," and "sub-stance," that communication must start if it is to occur at all.

The principal medium of symbolic action, language is always up for grabs, always the focus of conflict in a struggle over its meanings and uses, which we shape to accord with the conditions of our lives. For this reason, meanings change with changes in context; different groups can turn the "same" knowledge—the same texts, the same words—against one another, and "outsiders" can infuse a formerly alien language with their distinctive purposes and values. Burke himself gives the example of the Platonic dialogues, identified with conservative social interests during Plato's lifetime, but periodically appropriated by revolutionary forces during later periods of history (*Rhetoric of Motives* 28–29). He offers another example, however, which lies somewhat closer to home; closer, that is, to *our* order of motives:

> Indeed, two students, sitting side by side in a classroom where the principles of a specialized subject are being taught, can be expected to "identify" the subject differently, so far as its place in a total context is concerned. Many of the most important identifications for the specialty will not be established at all, until later in life, when the specialty has become integrally interwoven with the particulars of one's livelihood. (27)

Situating the lecture in different orders of motives, each of Burke's hypothetical students would construe it differently, and any communication between them about its implications would first require the search for a shareable sub-stance, a shareable ground of assumptions. These students might unexpectedly disagree, for example, about the meaning of an ordinary word in the lecture, a word like "rational." Possibly one would understand the term in its economic sense as a synonym for "cost-effective," while the other might associate "rational" with the idealist rigor of pure logic. Since both definitions are meaningful in different "orders," the two students could not continue their discussion until they found another term or constellation of terms still more basic than "rational" itself, upon which they might firmly establish their like-mindedness. By the same token, readers of this essay who are unfamiliar with Burke may perceive the preceding example as a kind of disruption, an act of violence, until they overcome through the struggle of interpretation the disparity between their presuppositions and mine. Beneath my intention to overturn the ideal of "clear writing," a reader might discover a motive we both share—the desire, perhaps, for a society less closed to unfamiliar voices.

For Burke, such a moment of discovery is clarity itself, which he does not oppose to imprecision or incorrectness, as teachers of freshman English might, but to "conspiracy," the suppression of the struggle essential to mutual understanding: thus his motto *Ad bellum purificandum* (*Rhetoric of Motives* 35). Just as injunctions against overt violence may perpetuate a subtler and more pervasive brutality, so there is a war that purifies and a peace that degrades. When in order to preserve such a degrading peace I ignore the social world behind the words of a student like Shawn, and when I therefore fail to assist him in the difficult activity of negotiation between his world and mine, I have committed an act of violence more destructive than any struggle aimed at the achievement of understanding. But the proponents of efficiency routinely engage in this verbal and conceptual eugenics as an aid to communication, a prerequisite to communality. What Burke maintains of "college education today in literature and the fine arts" holds no less true for the teaching of composition: "the very stress upon the pure autonomy of such activities is a roundabout way of identification with a privileged class" (*Rhetoric of Motives* 28). Burke suggests, in other words, that the fiction of good writing per se, or of clear thinking per se, always concedes to one group— and without a shot fired—the right to determine unilaterally the character of speech and reflection for everyone else.

Shots, however, are fired every day. Social life during the era of late capitalism has not been graced by the persistence of any single version of the truth, but is marked instead by a general state of discontinuity that would have been inconceivable even a century ago: an enormous proliferation of dissonant languages and values in the service of the "technological and commercial enterprise" (*Rhetoric of Motives* 30–31; *Grammar of Motives* 328). While Burke regards the struggle of communication as the search for a clarity "universal" by virtue of its inclusiveness, the exclusionary ideal of clarity we have inherited from the Progressive Era encourages us to act as though the Babel we now inhabit does not exist, and to see struggle as unnecessary, even downright antisocial (*Rhetoric of Motives* 35). The same forces which have banished private life from the "public" sphere maintain in the writing classroom the pretense of a common culture and a common language—maintain, it could be said, an image of ourselves exactly as we are *not*. "Clarity" has become an instrument of deception.

On the level of classroom practice there are no easy solutions to this institutional double bind. We disempower students by refusing to admit their language into our learned conversations, but we disempower them also by ignoring the demands of an educational apparatus which is decidedly not egalitarian and pluralistic—though it is still somewhat more so than the larger social order, where the standard of "good writing," like almost everything else, remains fundamentally unchanged from the days of Frank Presbrey. If we accept the normalization of public life as a *fait accompli*, we collude in excluding many important constituencies. (Consider the steady decline of minority enrollments nationwide and the high failure rates among those who continue to enroll). But if we challenge this normalization too openly, we ourselves risk being excluded by colleagues and administrators who regard "clarity" as the only legitimate concern of freshman English. I would argue, though, that the recognition of these conflicting imperatives can be a source of hidden strength, for our students as well as for us. When we imagine, on the contrary, that speech under the present conditions might unfold without struggle, then we have also been seduced by the illusion of efficiency, and we become seducers in turn. Rather than trying to protect students from the conflict which has given us our voices, we might do better to prepare them for it.

I believe that Irmscher has helped to prepare Shawn McGinnis for conflict by reading his essay rhetorically in the Burkean sense, as an attempt to "identify" our knowledge with his own social interests and to express those interests in the forum we now control. And I believe that by demystifying some of the conventions which govern our language practices he has encouraged Shawn to assume a position of authority within this forum: Shawn's weaknesses, as Irmscher demonstrates, involve commas and capitalization, not cognitive skills. Far from supporting the present order, Irmscher has abetted its future transformation by preserving the continuity, if only for one more person, between a world now vocal and a world now silent, or spoken of only by those to whom it does not belong. No less than students like Shawn, teachers who follow Irmscher's example, as I have tried to do in my classroom practice, are engaged in a war of communication. Together with our students we must resist an ever-widening disjunction between specialized discourse and the lived worlds we each inhabit. But simultaneously we must challenge—using all the available means of persuasion—the common sense of those colleagues whose failure to recognize any such disjunction has made academic knowledge useless, practically and politically, to everyone except a few specialists like themselves. While life beneath this two-bladed ax may seem from time to time unbearable, Irmscher and Burke both remind us that we cannot, except through struggle, pursue the ideal of a world in which struggle might become less necessary. Peace, as Burke says, is something we must fight for (*Grammar of Motives* 370).

Notes

1. Compare Johnson and Hartley's "revelation" (5) with Hirsch's in *Cultural Literacy:* "Recently, top executives of some large U.S.,

companies, including CBS and Exxon, met to discuss the fact that their younger middle-level executives could no longer communicate their ideas effectively in speech or writing" (5).

2. For this reading of Aristotle I am primarily indebted to Kenneth Burke's discussion of him in *A Rhetoric of Motives* (49–78) and also to Hans-Georg Gadamer's *Reason in the Age of Science,* especially 88–138. Neither author accepts the mythology of Athens as the "first democracy"; indeed, they both recognize that it was the need for persuasion which set relations among the city's free minority apart from all other social relations. Citizens were persuaded, foreigners coerced, slaves and servants compelled. In a democracy, where groups with widely disparate orientations meet on an equal footing, persuasion is often inadequate since it relies upon preexisting commonalities. Before one group can be persuaded by another, they must both achieve what Burke calls "identification," or what Gadamer describes as a "fusion of horizons."

2

*T*he Description of an Embarrassment: When Students Write about Religion

Chris Anderson

Not long ago, one of our teaching assistants brought me a paper that angered and upset her, one of the handful of "born-again" papers we get during a term. In it "Cathy" writes about her call to join a new church and how God has guided her every step of the way. The language is the language of the fundamentalist, of the testimonial, of *Guideposts* magazine and Sunday morning television:

> Christ died on the Cross for my sins [Cathy concludes].
> There is no way that I can repay Him for that, but I will
> try. I shall try to live my life fully for the Lord, and do
> His will. Hopefully, in doing this, I will also lead others
> to him. I know that this would make Him happy, because
> He loves every one of us and wants us to love Him and
> let Him come into our hearts.

The TA was offended by such talk and wanted my advice on whether she should mount some kind of frontal attack or restrain herself, and

This essay originally appeared in a slightly different form in the *ADE Bulletin* 94 (1989): 12–15.

the assumption was that I would share her disdain and embarrassment.

And I do. It's not just the simplicity and superficiality of the writing that bothers me. I'm bothered more by Cathy's assumption of authority, however mild, which is what I think most bothers all of us—not foolishness, but foolishness that is unaware of itself, superficiality that is either/or, dogmatic, unexamined. Maybe as academics we are especially uneasy about dogmatism in religion because we carry with us some ancestral memory of the time when the university was the handmaiden of the church, dominated by the church's patriarchal offices. But I'm bothered by exactly that attitude of unexamined authority in the teaching assistant as well. She assumes in this situation, without questioning, as if Moses brought them down from the mountain, the values of academic writing—complexity, proof, detachment, irony—assumes that these values are given, hold always. I hold to these values, too, as I will argue in the end, but my point here is that the TA hasn't *argued* them. In a sense she is just as dogmatic, just as privileging of a point of view, just as unaware of her own point of view as Cathy is. All discourse, she said to me, invoking the language of James Berlin's "social-epistemic" rhetoric, is the product of particular cultural and social influences, none of them sacrosanct, and our job is to make students like Cathy aware of these transactions, show them how meaning is always in flux, always changing, not fixed and immutable, not once and for all, as Cathy naively assumes. We need to teach Cathy that language creates us. Yes, I wanted to say, and as academics it's time that we were more aware that our own position is not beyond point of view.

I will admit to fictionalizing a little here, but only a little. The situation I've described is representative of issues that run deep in our teaching, issues that extend beyond the question of how students write about their religious experience.

Part of the problem in the scene I've described is that the teaching assistant has misread the real logic of "social-epistemic" rhetoric. That phrase, of course, comes from Berlin's recent essay in *College English,* "Rhetoric and Ideology in the Writing Class," a very useful and important essay because it captures so well the spirit of our profession now, the assumptions that are emerging as central and that graduate students and others like my TA are increasingly taking as given. It's a phrase I want to appropriate myself, even though I'm not entirely comfortable with it and want in fact to modify it in what I think are some important ways. Berlin's argument is that in a truer, more complete understanding of rhetoric, all language is recognized as intended, all acts of discourse as determined by place and time, as the products of a very delicate transaction among the writer, the reader, the subject, and the scene of the writing:

> For social-epistemic rhetoric, the real is located in a relationship that involves the dialectical interaction of the observer, the discourse community (social group) in which the observer is functioning, and the material conditions of existence. Knowledge is never found in any one of these but can only be posited as a product of the dialectic in which all three come together. (488)

The point is that no kind of language should be seen as necessarily superior to any other and that effective teaching and writing are always self-aware, in the act of examining their own assumptions. John Trimbur has written an important paper anticipating this argument in the context of what he calls "cultural studies." In an English curriculum built on the awareness of "ideology," according to Trimbur, the aim is to give students the intellectual tools to step back and examine the economic and social forces organizing their lives. This means, too, that all experience is seen as "text" to be interpreted, that literature is not defined as a sacred canon, and that composition is recognized as part of a wide spectrum of "textual studies," equal in importance to the others.

It seems to me that this view of rhetoric must, by definition, be open to the possibility of religious discourse. It is sometimes true that theorists like Berlin and Trimbur are absolutist in their antiabsolutism, blind, like my teaching assistant, to their own bias. In their zeal to expose the givens, the unsupportable premises, on which all philosophical systems depend, they sometimes seem to be unaware of how their critical method has itself become dogmatic, how method has acquired a moral force—as method, as if there is only method. But that blindness isn't necessary in the logic of this approach as I understand it. A truly "ironic" and open-ended view of rhetoric like the one Berlin and Trimbur profess cannot exclude the possibility of transcendence, because transcendence is something we sometimes think we experience and because to exclude transcendence would be to set up a contradictory and tyrannous harmony. It is true that the religious rhetoric of Cathy and the other born-again writers is "Neoplatonic" or "expressionistic," in Berlin's terms, since it assumes the existence of an authentic self and an authentic experience in some way outside or in excess of language and so, according to Berlin, oversimplifies, falsifies, the complexity of meaning. Yet if Berlin and the others are really serious in their demand for critical detachment, they need—and we need—to give even Cathy's rhetoric its due. The irony must cut both ways to have real validity.

If I am right about this, a genuinely social-epistemic response to Cathy's paper would be more layered and complicated than the instinctive response of my TA. First, we need to make Cathy more self-conscious, more self-aware; we could ask her to examine her assumptions. We should take this as a teachable moment, perhaps ask her to rewrite the paper with an audience of outsiders in mind, confronting the rhetorical problems that such an audience creates, or reflecting on the difficulty of expressing religious belief in contemporary America. But, at the same time, as instructors we also need to understand that academic language is not the only language. Cathy's rhetoric *is* appropriate in other settings, as testimonial during a church meeting, in prayer discussions, and so on. It is a kind of code, produced by and proper in certain situations; her problem is that she's applied this code to the wrong situation, not that she's used a wrong code. To put this another way, Cathy has the right to her own voice, even though we can and should argue for the value of the voice *we* are trying to teach her.

Moreover, we need to appreciate the extreme rhetorical difficulty Cathy and any religious writer faces. Theology is "the description of an embarrassment," the theologian Karl Barth says (102). Faith is a matter of intuiting the inexplicable and of making a leap that cannot be justified to anyone who hasn't made that leap. And as if the pressure of wordlessness were not enough, the Christian rhetorician must operate in the midst of two thousand years of cliché, so that at the mere mention of *Christian* catchphrases, doors slam shut all over the place. We need simply to appreciate that difficulty, tell Cathy and the others we appreciate it.

I would go even further. Religious rhetoric is the ideal way of examining the assumptions of all discourse, is an ideal test case, because in it the kinds of bias that are present in all language are especially evident because especially blatant. All rhetoric (here I am expressing what I take to be the main tenet of social-epistemic rhetoric) is an effort to magnify the presence of a priori assumptions that cannot themselves be justified, that are somehow assumed, are somehow leaps, faiths. The realm of rhetoric is the realm of faith in this sense, as James Kinneavy argues in *The Greek Rhetorical Roots of Early Christian Faith* (135–37) and Kenneth Burke before him in *A Rhetoric of Motives* (51–52). Thus, Faith with a capital F can illustrate with special power the operations, the structure, the logic, of the faith of *pistis*, of proof seen as some kind of leap. I propose, then, putting together a unit on religious discourse as part of a composition class—various readings on religious rhetoric, from Hadden and Swann's *Prime Time Preachers* to Neil Postman's *Amusing Ourselves to Death* to selections from the writing of Frederick Buechner and others[1]—and then asking students to write about their own religious background and experience from a social-epistemic point of view, as I've appropriated that term. Berlin uses as an example of effective pedagogy Ira Shor's strategy of having students write about the operations of McDonald's or Burger King (see his *Critical Teaching and Everyday Life* 114). Surely religious experience is at least as interesting from a cultural point of view as the production of Big Macs or Whoppers.

I don't mean to suggest that we should go about all this in an entirely "critical" way, in the negative sense of that term, because that would be too easy, and it would involve us in another layer of contradiction and irony. I agree with Wayne Booth that it's far too easy to talk always about "our freedom from" restraint and illusion and that for culture to keep going we also need to talk about our "freedom to"—our freedom to make commitments and accept value, however provisionally (147). Annie Dillard's wonderful essay "Singing with the Fundamentalists" is one model of the kind of writing and the kind of critical perspective—the balancing act—I'm recommending. For weeks a group of fundamentalists had gathered around a fountain underneath Dillard's office window to pray and sing hymns, and one day, despite her uneasiness, she went down and joined them. And then she found herself singing with them every week:

> All around me, eyes are closed and hands are raised. There is no social pressure to do this, or anything else. I've never known any group to be less cohesive, imposing fewer controls. Since no one looks at anyone, and since passersby no longer look, everyone out here is inconspicuous and free. Perhaps the palm-raising has begun because the kids realize by now that they are not on display: they're

praying in their closets, right out here on the Square. . . .
The sun is rising higher. We are singing our last song.
We are praying. We are alone together. (202)

What I admire about this essay is Dillard's tough-minded, truly
critical, intellectual refusal to make judgments about the singing
fundamentalists or to rely on the convenient stereotypes I know I
rely on too often. Dillard brings us all up short, I think, because she
has the discipline and the critical detachment actually to enter into
the experience of the fundamentalists without denying its validity,
even though in the end she does implicitly question its intellectual
depth. What she discovers is that some of the easy generalizations
about "fundamentalists" as a group are simply wrong: the individuals
who come are too varied in background, levels of ability, degrees of
conservatism or liberalism. What she discovers is that her colleagues
looking down on them from the windows of the offices above are
imprisoned behind the glass in their own points of view, absolutist
in their antiabsolutism. What I admire about the Dillard essay is her
courage in risking embarrassment. I admire the essay as writing: its
concreteness, its dramatization of process and thus complexity, its
autobiographical frame and thus its admission of bias, or in social-
epistemic terms, of ideology.

As another model I would offer a paper written by a student in
one of my introduction to poetry classes. I had asked the class to
imagine writing a letter to a friend or relative trying to persuade that
person to read one of the poems we had discussed. The topic was an
effort to get students to think about their conflicting audiences and
the real value, for them, of the poetry we'd been reading. Colleen
wrote a paper in response to Hopkins's great poem "The Windhover,"
which I had used both as a good example, because extreme, of what
all poetic language does—condense, intensify, warp—and as an effort
to subvert Christian cliché, attack easy armchair Christianity. I presented the poem rhetorically. Hopkins, I claimed, used this strange,
warped, intensified, I think wonderful language as an indirect, shock-
ing way of defamiliarizing the kinds of homilies we slam doors on.
He was trying to preach to us, but without seeming to.

I find Colleen's response powerful and moving, the description
not of an embarrassment but of an engagement—self-aware without
being cynical, aware of complexity. Here's how she describes her
experience with Hopkins' language:

To fully appreciate this poem, you have to read it out-
loud. Your tongue will struggle with words like "daylight's dauphin, dapple-dawn-drawn" and "skate's heel
sweeps smooth." Your brain will struggle to understand
the words we no longer use. The poem was written so
the reader would struggle, just as the bird does. Hopkins,
a nineteenth century poet, used even older language so
his peers would have the same struggle with understanding the words that we do today. And as he describes the
struggle of the bird in terms of brute beauty, reading this
poem has that beautiful struggle. It isn't like most of the
poems that flow easily and speak of lovely things.

She then goes on to apply the notion of effort and struggle to
her experience growing up in a Pentecostal church, converting to
Mormonism, then becoming disillusioned with the Mormons:

Through my inner struggle, I discovered my own
strength, and a feeling of connectedness with all hu-
mankind that led me to the belief of a God within. This
belief took years of anguish and work to develop, and it
is this struggle that I can identify with in "The Windhover." The line, "the achieve of, the mastery of the
thing," describes my sense of accomplishment in over-
coming my fears of God, and the acceptance of God
in my life. . . . Coming to accept and love myself as an
individual with imperfections has been a struggle of "glid-
ing" and being "rebuffed by the wind."

What I admire about Colleen's response to Hopkins is her ability to
read her own experience in terms of the poem, to use the poem's
complexity and tension as a way of clarifying her own conflict and
mastery. I admire her grasp of the poem's important lesson about the
uncertainty and difficulty of any act of faith.

But Colleen's paper raises a final problem, a problem not in the
sense that it's bad or avoidable but in the sense that it's part of the
infinite regress of this whole issue. I agree with the social-epistemic
rhetoricians that we think in language, so that—in the logic of this
argument—if we change the *way* students write, change their language, we also change *what* they think, what it is possible for them
to think. If form is the shape of content, content is the shape of form.

The question is: if we teach students complexity and irony in form, if we teach them the values of academic writing, are we not then changing the way they think? If we teach them to write with complexity about their religious experience, for example, are we not then changing their faith—not giving them the right to their own language but implicitly and explicitly offering a model of what we think of as a better, because more sophisticated, understanding of religious experience?

This is what I think I've done with Colleen, even though I was also careful to acknowledge her right to speak and write elsewhere in the voice of her childhood religious tradition. In class I argued that "The Windhover" describes the private moment of epiphany—of revelation, of Hopkins seeing the hawk, the windhover, fighting against the wind—as if it were the text of grace and as if that text is not certain but fleeting, distant, full of various meanings, hard to read. The theme of the poem is that religious experience is like a difficult language. The bird is like Christ but only momentarily, with violence, energy, ambiguity. I argued that the language of the poem, in its complexity and nuances, acts out that theme—that in our efforts to figure out this rich, textured, sprung language, we, too, have to fight against the wind. Finally—and this is how I use literature to teach composition—I argued that these values, both stylistic and religious, are also the values that make good writing, that Hopkins in an extreme way is doing what students should do: acknowledging complexity, seeing both sides, all sides, even while maintaining a focus, that he is seeing outside himself and doubting even while he is believing, and that in his radical particularity he is justifying, documenting, proving, as best he can, his thesis: the glory of God.

Colleen has obviously been persuaded by my "flying against the wind" sermon, and she is able to act out her understanding in her prose. Haven't I influenced the way she believes, the quality, the character, of her belief? In getting her to see the language of the poem in this way, and then getting her to see her own language on this model, haven't I made Jonathan Livingston Seagull into the windhover?

I don't ask this as a way of confessing uneasiness or contradiction, but more as a way of saying that we are all of us, as teachers of writing and literature, always in the business of recommending values, insisting on faiths. My faith is in analysis, irony, self-examination, applied to religious experience as to anything else. My faith is in complexity, complexity which is complex enough not to deny the possibility of any origin, and this complexity, I think, can best be brought to us in language, and in literary language in particular.

To return, then, to my paraphrase of social-epistemic rhetoric: I would say that what we should be teaching is not merely a critical attitude toward value and commitment. Instead, we should be teaching our students to recognize the fact that we are, all of us and everywhere, continually engaged in the search for values and the making of commitments.

The difference in tone between these two statements is crucial, finally a statement of value itself, as applicable, I think, to essays about hamburgers as to essays about hawks that fly against the wind.

Note

1. See, for example, Buechner's *The Alphabet of Grace, The Sacred Journey,* and *Now and Then,* three powerful examples of creative nonfiction about religious experience. For an analysis of Buechner's nonfiction and the rhetorical problems of faith, see my "The Very Style of Faith: Frederick Buechner as Homilist and Essayist."

3

*R*hetorics of the Self

Mary Louise Buley-Meissner

> The word *rhetoric* can be traced back ultimately to the simple assertion *I say.*
>
> —Young, Becker, and Pike

Only two words: "I say." Yet in that statement can be found the beginning of rhetoric: the desire to speak as an individual, to express a personal point of view. In "Why I Write," Joan Didion observes, "I write entirely to find out what I'm thinking, what I'm looking at, what I see and what it means." Similarly, Annie Dillard places *I* at the center of all her writing. As she says in "Seeing," "It's all a matter of keeping my eyes open" (17), a process of clarifying and questioning the perceptions shaping her sense of reality. Writing focuses thoughts, connects ideas, constructs the images that construct reality—and identity. Through language, the *I* becomes apparent; *the self* takes shape. Through language, having a point of view becomes possible. Like many contemporary essayists, Didion and Dillard insist upon the self-expressive and self-creative nature of their work.

Yet recent composition and literary theory suggests that the *I* of written discourse is an illusion, that it represents neither an enduring sense of self nor a definitively individual way of looking at the world. For example, from a deconstructive perspective "the writer is understood as the product of a system of conventions that operates outside of her control. Thus everything, including the self of the writer, is considered to be fiction, everything is considered to be text" (Shelly

1). Based on that perspective, a recent textbook cautions students: "We often think of ourselves as individuals, with . . . an 'essential' nature that is 'ours.' But we are all produced by society's distinctive ideology, constituted by the many discourses of society" (McCormick, Waller, and Flower 290). In typical conclusion to that argument, teachers and students alike are urged to recognize that "social theories of reading and writing have helped to deconstruct the myth of the autonomous essential self" (Joseph Harris 20).

If indeed "the myth" of individual self-definition has been exposed, then what does the *I* of written discourse represent? And how is it composed? These questions matter because our answers largely determine what we teach, how we teach, and why.

Essentially, concepts of *the self* are important because they affirm the value of corresponding *rhetorics of the self.* For example, if we define the self in terms of its expressiveness and creativity, then we are likely to value and encourage the development of a personal voice, an ethos of personal integrity, and writing that demonstrates originality. But if we define the self in terms of its linguistic and social construction, then we may be much more interested in examining the forces that make any *I* an object as well as a subject of discourse. In general, different concepts of the self lead to different ways of imagining the relationships between writer, reader, subject, and reality. As James Berlin notes in *Rhetoric and Reality,* "A particular rhetoric . . . instructs students about the nature of general knowledge, or truth. . . . The nature of truth will in turn determine the roles of [the writer and reader] in discovering and communicating it" (4). Perhaps most importantly, rhetorics guide intellectual inquiry, setting (and sometimes extending) boundaries for exploring the new, the uncertain, the unknown.

Any such inquiry, I would suggest, begins with and returns to the self—a unique intersection of history, language, culture, and individual experience. Every act of writing can be seen as an act of self-representation, as an attempt to shape the words and thoughts giving rise to our consciousness of who we are. Yet "who we are" keeps changing, keeps complicating. Our understanding of "who we are" is always incomplete. Neither the full complexity nor the open-ended uncertainty of our experience can ever be completely captured by our writing. As I tell my students, there can never be an equivalence between *the self writing* and *the self being written* into their texts. Furthermore, it is the self being written into their texts that will interest their readers—if only because it is on the page, accessible, open to question.

And so when I use the term *rhetorics of the self,* I mean rhetorics of the textual self, the deliberately constructed self. How do students represent their concerns? How do they try to persuade their readers to see the world from their point of view? Particularly within the context of the university, how do they negotiate the relationship between the self writing and the self being written?

Answers to these questions largely depend on the rhetorics of the self that students use to claim their places in our classrooms. For example, in "Inventing the University" David Bartholomae observes that many basic writers try to "write their way into the university" by using a "conventional rhetoric of the self" (15), relying on assertions of sincerity and originality to carry out their arguments. The *I* of their discourse seems far removed from the self-creative *I* of a Didion or Dillard, perhaps closer to the fictitious *I* recognized by deconstructionists. In my view, however, the *I* of their discourse represents an uneasy alliance between two classical models of self-representation that many students acquire in college preparatory writing classes, namely, the Platonic idealist and the Aristotelian pragmatist.

Each of these models allows an individual different possibilities for making a personal point of view convincing to others, different strategies for claiming the authority to speak publicly. In the discourse of the idealist, the *I* is made to seem transparent, so that an audience can imagine seeing through it to the speaker himself; often in the most convincing arguments, the sincerity of the *I* and the speaker seem to coincide. Following this model, students may not be able to make any distinction between the self writing and the self written. Accordingly, they may try to build their arguments on popular wisdom and generalizations ("as we all know") meant to ensure the goodwill of their readers. In the discourse of the pragmatist, however, the *I* is deliberately made oblique; rather than revealing the speaker's character, it commonly reflects the audience's. Influenced by this model, students are likely to be more concerned with affirming their readers' beliefs than with presenting their own. Assuming the self writing and the self written to be completely separate, they may substitute empty abstractions for their own ideas (often as if they are trying to imitate what they do not yet understand). In addition, under the pressure of examination, students are likely to try working from one model, then from another, producing abrupt, confusing shifts in point of view. What basic writers and many other students fail to recognize is that the *I* of their discourse cannot be fixed on the page. As James Miller, Jr., observes, we all "liv[e] and breath[e] in a linguistic environment" with a "ceaseless flow of language" surrounding and moving through us (18). The self writing cannot stop that flow, but it can allow an *I* to emerge from the "interior stream of language" (18) shaping our individuality. The self written into any one text is thus written out of a larger text (linguistic consciousness) making both identity (self-knowledge) and community (shared meaning) possible. Neither equivalent nor divided, the self writing and the self written are in continual interplay. Paradoxically, an *I* acknowledging its own tentativeness, its own temporality, may be much more convincing than an *I* presented as fixed on the page, completed with its last word.

Consider, for example, the *I* presented in "Optical Illusions," an essay by one of my students in English 201, Strategies for Academic Writing (see appendix 3–1 for the complete essay). In conference, Kevin had said that Didion could write about only one subject (herself), while Dillard could write about many subjects; it seemed "right" to him to define them as completely "different writers" on that basis. After being asked to reconsider his point of view, Kevin began his analysis of their essays with this statement: "One of the hardest things for me to do is admit I was wrong, but that's what I've got to do."

Kevin uses a rhetoric of the self that seems to conflate the self writing and the self written—a rhetoric that traps him in literality. The self written into his text is helpless, without options, a version of the student self that conforms to the teacher's expectations. Part of the problem is Kevin's resistance to reading the essays assigned in class (signaled in his second sentence by his reference to essays he "had to" read). More importantly, however, his approach to writing is bound to the factual, to what can be proved conclusively right or wrong—an approach he uses to show why Didion and Dillard cannot be considered "different writers" after all.

For example, in "Section One: I Thought," Kevin demonstrates his understanding of Dillard's "Sojourner" by recording what he considers to be the most important facts of her essay: "Mangrove trees grow to be 5 to 6′ tall. They grow in rows 25 to 30′ to the left or right of other trees . . . " and so on. In Kevin's rhetoric of accuracy, these facts are used to prove that he has read "Sojourner" carefully. But they are taken from an encyclopedia (not Dillard's essay), and they obscure the metaphoric nature of her imagery. Similarly, Kevin goes on to list situations drawn from his own experience, such as "being alone in a state where you have no relatives," to show that he knows what Dillard means by loneliness—thereby missing the multileveled meaning of her theme. His later treatment of Didion's "Goodbye to All That" is much the same, relying on facts about New York and the current employment market to prove that her main theme is "We've all done things we regret."

Ironically, the credibility of the *I* in his discourse is undermined by its own insistence on being correct. For example, in "Section Two: The Teacher Suggested," Kevin records the teacher's advice verbatim, carefully placing it in quotation marks. But the advice itself—"If I were you, I wouldn't take what Didion or Dillard says literally"—is ignored. In the last section of his essay, "The End of It," Kevin is back where he started: "Now that I think about it, I was wrong when I said Didion and Dillard are different writers. . . . Didion and Dillard are the same." By this reductive logic, *all* writers who deal with common human experiences become "the same."

Geoffrey Chase suggests that when "the process of instruction breaks down," teachers need to reconsider "what students are being asked, explicitly and implicitly, to learn" (14). In effect, Kevin was being asked to reconceptualize the *I* of his discourse. Instead he normalized it, made it as "obvious" as his readings of "Sojourner" and "Goodbye to All That." Like the *I* of his discourse, *Didion* and *Dillard* label what has yet to be closely examined or understood. Consequently, the self written into his text has no questions to ask; its rhetoric is completely declarative—and finally unconvincing.

Looking at the work of students such as Kevin, I recognize that concepts of the self may be shaped by forces more complex than personal understanding (or misunderstanding) of the kinds of self-representation that writing makes possible. Students act out concepts that they have acquired from teachers, but neither they nor their teachers often stop to identify or examine the concepts in a social-historical framework. For example, when students limit themselves to recording facts about a subject rather than interpreting its meaning—as Kevin does in "Optical Illusions"—they are acting much as students did in composition classes more than fifty years ago. Indeed, the early history of freshman writing programs suggests that composition instruction often has had a powerful normalizing, *self*-limiting function.

For example, from 1920 to 1940, when the first freshman writing programs were being organized, scientific concepts of the self, drawn from behavioral and social science, stressed understanding individual differences in terms of group norms. As Berlin explains in *Rhetoric and Reality* (chap. 4), empirical methods of assessing students' writing skills were widespread at that time, including placement tests, grammar-usage exams, objective scales for grading essays, and exit exams. Writing programs at large state universities commonly grouped students by ability level in classes emphasizing practice in arrangement and style. Invention usually was not taught, mainly because the content of writing was not considered problematic. In general, students were trained to become objective observers and accurate recorders of an external reality that was fixed according to its own rules. Thus, basic assumptions concerning the self, writing, and reality all served utilitarian aims. What kind of student was best suited for a college education? What methods of instruction were most likely to ensure the acquisition of essential writing skills? What kind of educational system would best promote American ideals? All of these questions could be answered in terms of group standards, objective criteria, and public agreement on the need for a more highly trained business class to manage the country's economy.

Guided by scientific assumptions regarding the self as observer, students fifty years ago were trained to take a factual point of view, to use language to record the "obvious." At the same time, students frequently found themselves under examination—their abilities measured, their accomplishments quantified. Essentially, the self as observer was not separated from the self observed; both were empirically defined. The work of students like Kevin, students who struggle to be "correct" in their teachers' eyes, suggests that definitions of academic achievement are highly resistant to change.

Also powerful to this day are functional concepts of the self, dominant from 1940 to 1960 during the era of general education (see Rudolph). At that time, research in linguistics (especially semantics) supported the establishment of interdepartmental, skills-oriented courses to meet the needs of students from widely varied backgrounds. With college and university enrollments climbing after World War II, such courses seemed especially useful in the rebuilding of a peacetime economy. Writing, reading, speaking, and listening all were taught as skills to be practiced and improved so that students could function efficiently in society. The practical aims of higher education also were underscored by the establishment of the Conference on College Composition and Communication in 1949, when lessons in composition became synonymous with lessons in grasping the basic tools of communication (e.g., vocabulary, grammar, practical forms of composition) that would enable students to express their ideas in socially acceptable ways. Consequently, the self as communicator seemed inseparable from the self communicated—both being judged according to public standards of competency (as defined by placement and exit exams typical of writing programs a generation before).

Overall, concepts of the self, writing, and reality from 1940 to 1960 reinforced each other much as they had in earlier years. In writing programs guided by functional assumptions of the self as communicator, students acquired the skills they needed to keep society operating smoothly. As in earlier programs influenced by scientific perceptions of the self as observer, higher education was viewed as utilitarian; students were prepared to assume productive roles in a reality that was economically defined. Accordingly, composition instruction may have served to normalize not only students' language, but also their self-expectations as language users.

Like students forty years ago, many students today are highly influenced by functional concepts of the self as communicator. In their perspective, writing requires following conventional forms of arrangement and style—including forms of self-representation that often reduce the *I* of their discourse to a pronoun without any definite referent. Consider, for example, the insubstantiality of the *I* in "One Freshman's Adjustment" (appendix 3–2) by Beth, a 201 student who seems to separate the self written from the self writing in order to complete her model of the perfect five-paragraph theme.

Beth uses a rhetoric of the self that seems paradoxical. The word *I* appears twenty-nine times in thirty-four sentences, yet the self written into her text is voiceless, anonymous: "I thought . . . I guess I didn't really know . . . I felt . . ." But thought what in particular? Beth does not explain because the ethos of her rhetoric depends on erasing her individuality. She constructs a self whose only claim to authority is knowing what she supposes "everyone knows." Moreover, this self is not a subject, but rather the object of events and experiences that Beth can only record, not question.

Indeed, from the first sentence on her rhetoric closes off questioning: "The transition from high school to college affected my life profoundly." Through the rest of the essay, Beth follows a predictable pattern. Change happens to Beth, takes her through college, lets her find out what "everyone knows." Her descriptions of dorm life, partying, and studying emphasize that she is unexceptional, "pretty human," thinking and acting as other college students do. Inevitably, she reaches the conclusion that "my horizons were broadened by college. . . . My social life . . . changed. . . . It was a profound change." As her use of passive voice suggests, perhaps Beth has yet to conceive of the self (writing or written) as an active construct. Many teachers would say Beth's essay is too personal, too self-centered. My analysis is that in spite of all the references to *I*, the essay is impersonal, other-centered, ego-less. Yet I puzzle over statements such as these: "Everyone knows how hard it is to say 'no' to something they really want to do and 'yes' to something that they *have* to do" and "I thought, well, I'll find time to study later this week or tomorrow when nothing is going on." In such statements, I locate the tension of the essay: although Beth's subject is "One Freshman's Adjustment" to college, she presents a self that has not adjusted—except in the most superficial ways—and actually resists adjustment.

Confronted by such writing, we need to consider carefully how we would like it to change. Should Beth reframe her writing to push the first-person *I* out to the margins? Or should she bring that *I* to the center, where it can be examined and questioned? To become more compelling, perhaps Beth's writing first has to become more personal, more particularized, more open about its own devaluing of academic life.

As Ann Berthoff observes, "Rhetoric reminds us that the function of language is not only to name, but also to *formulate* and to *transform*—to give form to feeling, cogency to argument, shape to memory" ("Problem Solving" 647). The function of *I* is no different. It not only names, but also transforms the entire complex of feelings, beliefs, and relationships that it represents. In Beth's discourse, whenever *I* is inserted, it reduces her experience to an imitation of College Life. But rather than simply removing it, perhaps she needs to work at remaking it in terms of her own doubts about the demands being placed on her.

Doing so, however, would be risky for her. Much as we may want our students to achieve "a personal investment" in their writing (Annas 369), they often are convinced that the best writing is the most predictable. As Les Perelman notes, "In institution-based discourse both speaker and hearer exist largely as projections of institutional roles rather than as idiosyncratic individuals" (474). Education then becomes a process of conforming to those roles, rather than questioning or attempting to redefine them, as Bartholomae makes clear:

> To speak with authority student writers not only have to
> speak in another's voice but through another's "code";
> and they not only have to do this, they have to speak in
> the voice and through the codes of those of us with power
> and wisdom; and they not only have to do this, they have
> to do it before they know what they are doing, before
> they have a project to participate in and before, at least
> in terms of our discipline, they have anything to say.
> ("Inventing" 17)

Is this truly "to speak with authority"—to speak in another's voice, without understanding, without having anything to say? Bartholomae's description of academic discourse suggests that many teachers and students believe it is. If it is, then the self writing and the self written are both likely to remain products of the university, rather than producers of ideas and questions that might lead to new formulations of the "codes" (especially the discursive practices) defining students' educational possibilities.

But suppose that "to speak with authority" means something quite different. Suppose that it means developing an individual voice, questioning what is not understood, even undermining the idea that "those of us with power and wisdom" are models for students to imitate. Then education could become a process of self-affirmation, engaging students in making the connections—between the personal and the academic, between who they are and who they are becoming—that could strengthen their ability to succeed at whatever "project" they might choose to undertake.

In my view, developing a *self*-conscious voice enables students to participate in the kind of dialogue essential to progressive education—dialogue that places students in active, critical relationship to teachers, texts, institutions (including the university), history, culture. As Henry Giroux and Peter McLaren emphasize, voice needs to be understood as "the discursive means by which students . . . attempt to make themselves 'heard' and to define themselves as active authors of their world" (235). Essentially, having a voice enables an individual to resist being silenced, to resist being made anonymous.

Moreover, I recognize that developing a voice, composing a self, and constructing knowledge are remarkably similar processes, all of them involving the integration of private and public dimensions of experience. For example, in writing across the disciplines, a student's voice becomes stronger as his or her language taps deeper, self-achieved understanding of a subject. Yet what we know and how we know it are never entirely decided by ourselves; instead, the subjects and methods of our inquiry are largely determined by what others have done before us (e.g., writers in a given field) and by what others would like us to do (e.g., teachers in a given discipline). To make ourselves heard, we need to understand what has already been said. Distinctly personal, a voice nonetheless is social in origin.

Similarly, the self that we identify as our own does not exist in solitude. Our self-perceptions are highly influenced by others' perceptions; to a certain extent, we know "who we are" because of the ways that others have defined us. Family, friends, social class, race, religion—all of these speak through and about us in our discourse. Yet language enables us to articulate our differences from others as well as our similarities; it allows us to examine and reflect on the process of our self-formation. Personally sustained and socially engaged, the self that we identify as our own resists any final definition.

Constructing knowledge—like developing a voice and composing a self—depends on achieving a sense of *connectedness,* an awareness of the interrelationships between personal and social experience, identity and community, who we are and who we are becoming. As Mary Belenky and her colleagues emphasize in *Women's Ways of Knowing,* active understanding of any subject depends on integrating knowledge intuitively felt to be important with knowledge learned from others (134). Moreover, they argue that "answers to all questions vary depending on the context in which they are asked and on the frame of reference of the person doing the asking" (137). As many cultural studies suggest, the knowledge that any one person (or society) holds can be only an approximation of knowledge—never the truth, but always a tentative configuration of truth. And nowhere is that as evident as it is in writing.

As Phyllis McCord emphasizes, teachers and students alike need to see writing "not as [an attempt] to capture or mirror an objective reality, but as efforts to produce a plausible, convincing version of ideas and events, of which there are many other possible versions" (751). The writing of another student, Michael, has made me see how exciting—and *self-*extending—that enterprise can be.

In "Collage: 1972" (appendix 3–3), Michael develops an exploratory rhetoric of the self that I find intriguing. The first sentence of the opening section, "Before," establishes the ironic doubleness of the narrator's voice, situation, and point of view: "Looking up from my Matchbox toy cars, I saw the bodies leaving Vietnam on our

T.V., bagged and stacked like trash on the curb." This self stands as a witness to history in at least two ways: seeing as a child, and reseeing as an adult, violent tragedies of war, protest, and assassination. Moreover, the *I* of this discourse seems to represent an intersection of the self writing (Michael remembering the past) and the self written (Michael remembered). It is an *I* aware of its own tentativeness, its own possibilities for being shaped in other ways.

Consider, for example, the *I* of the following sequence: "I saw the waves of police and National Guard sweep across the screen, truncheons swinging freely, people crumbling and stumbling under their boots. And the fire hoses, as if the crowd could be doused and extinguished and washed away like dirt off a driveway." Whose perspective is being shaped here—the naive child's? The outraged adult's? Both? Or consider this simple statement: "I remember the world in that little box spilling into our home." Where is the line separating observation from interpretation, memory from imagination? Michael's writing suggests that the line is elusive, no more definite than the boundary between fact and fiction.

Some teachers might say that "Collage: 1972" is no more than "creative writing." But in my estimation, it is nothing less. As the work of many contemporary essayists suggests, all writing is fiction, always an attempt to tell a truth that remains elusive, beyond any final understanding. Similarly, Michael's writing is creative because his rhetoric of the self is based on an understanding of language as creative. Rather than acting out traditional concepts of the self as observer or the self as communicator, Michael explores the possibilities of the self as symbolizer, as a maker of meaning that is open to interpretation.

For example, rather than assuming the innocence of the child in "Collage: 1972," Michael makes the following statement an important part of his rhetorical frame: "Sometimes it's as though I have betrayed my generation, my descendants, my ancestors, by not caring about the bullets and bombs in the world, by running my toy cars up and down the carpet while our black and white Zenith exploded with violence." Where does innocence end and culpability begin? In Michael's writing, his way of asking the question becomes a way of beginning to answer it.

"Collage: 1972" also engages my interest because it invites rereading. Rather than defining itself as "student writing," its form is open-ended. For example, only after several readings did I realize that the events of ten years pass by while the child continues to play in front of the television. Time stops as the narrator describes news broadcasts of the 1960s and the 1970s. But the broadcasts are no more realistic than the rest of the scene. Like "the bright yellows and reds" of the cars, "the gray blood and tears" on the television are colored by cultural memory of innocence and loss. Reading "Collage: 1972," I realize how powerful that memory can be.

Is this writing "personal" or "academic"—or both? Is Michael writing to himself, his generation, or a much wider audience? The rhetoric of the self at the center of Michael's writing is too complex for easy answers. By presenting his readers with a first-person narrator, Michael draws us into seeing through the narrator's eyes. But when the narrator's identity slips away, we are left with our own: "*I* saw the bodies leaving Vietnam . . . *I* saw the waves of police and National Guard . . . " (emphasis added). Yes, I saw. And what was my response? That is what Michael seems to be asking me through his writing, through his use of a rhetoric that depends not simply on an ethos of mutual understanding, but on a shared awareness of moral ambiguity.

In the next section of Michael's essay, "During," his rhetoric of the self draws us further into his writing. The initial sentence suggests a change of perspective: "When I became a swimmer, I packed away my Matchbox cars on basement shelves." What does it mean to be a swimmer? At first, it seems to be associated with patriotism, with the red, white, blue, and gold of the Olympics—much in contrast to the gray and white television pictures of the essay's opening section. But the narrator goes on to remind us that eleven athletes were murdered at the Olympics by "faceless armed men" and an "unreal world which could only reach me through that little box and picture tube." To be a swimmer does not offer any escape from the violence that the narrator turned away from as a child. Instead, he must confront the fact that "over Vietnam, Andy Pick [another swimmer] was killed." Death on the ground, death in the skies: the absurdity of it is inarguable, mocking the narrator's own ambition. But he simply states, "Some dreams have time bombs."

Then comes the scene that I find most interesting in the whole essay. At the Junior Olympics, the narrator has his moment of glory, experiences his still point in the turning world: "The sound of the crowd vanished, and for that instant of silence and stillness there was clarity: internal, singular, and complete. The earth had ceased turning to give me a moment to understand." In *Metaphors of the Self,* James Olney comments:

> Any understanding of God and His universe, or the laws
> of the natural world, or the structure of human society,
> must come out of and will inevitably be deeply colored
> by the nature of the self and the knowledge that one has
> of that self lying at the center, and being the very heart,
> of the understanding that one comes to. (13)

In "Collage: 1972," understanding seems to depend on finding ways to focus experience that would otherwise be overwhelming. For example, being *in* the race, being totally concentrated on his own efforts is what matters to the narrator—not winning, not outdistancing anyone else. Moreover, Michael's rhetoric of the self makes me see the swimmer as a symbol of the writer—an individual immersed in language as we all are, but also an individual who makes that language his element, who dives deep to discover the meanings made possible by words.

As Michael suggests in the last section of his essay, "After," swimming—like writing—allows exploration of known and unknown realms of experience, enabling us to extend our understanding of who we are and what we can be. With that understanding, we can shape much more than our own identities. As Michael observes in the last sentence of his essay: "We can collage a universe from the images of our past, our present and our future."

Recent research on discourse communities has emphasized that students need to move from being "outsiders" to "insiders" and that their writing needs to break away from the personal in order to become academically acceptable. "Authentic voice" pedagogy has been criticized for its self-centeredness, while collaborative learning has been advocated on the basis that all knowledge is a social construction, that the group—rather than the individual—decides meaning. As a result, I see a separation being made between the personal self and the academic self, between writing for oneself and writing for an audience, between personally achieved understanding and academically valued knowledge. But I want to resist that separation.

Is Michael's writing, for example, that of an "outsider" or an "insider"? I cannot find a thesis in it. I do not know if this work shows he can go on to write an acceptable essay for any other teacher. But his writing keeps me in it. It gives meaning to his experience, and in that way, I think, enlarges my own sense of reality.

In *Tough, Sweet, and Stuffy,* Walker Gibson remarks that "by looking at rhetoric, we may begin to know who it is we are making believe we are. And then, perhaps, we can do something about it" (87). By looking at the rhetorics of the self in my students' writing, I try to understand who they imagine themselves to be as composers. As they act out concepts of the self and try out possibilities of being observers or communicators or symbolizers, I see them doing much more than "making believe." I see them discovering that ways of using language can become ways of making—or remaking—belief itself. Isn't belief made possible by vision? And isn't vision made possible by the *I* open to the new, the uncertain, the unknown? "This looking business is risky," Dillard reminds us ("Seeing" 23). We never can be certain of what we will find or of how our discoveries will change us. After looking at students' writing for many years, I am no longer certain of what "student writing" should be. Should it be clear, correct, organized? Should it be complex, engaging, thought-provoking? Can it be both? All I know is that *the self*— expressed, shaped, constructed, created—is at the center of writing that matters to me, that makes me reenvision the world.

Appendix 3–1: "Optical Illusion" in Three Sections

The Beginning

One of the hardest things for me to do is admit I was wrong, but that's what I've got to do. When I started reading the essays I had to read to write this essay, I thought Joan Didion and Annie Dillard were different writers. It seemed clear to me from what I'd read, Joan Didion could only write about one subject, while Annie Dillard could write about many different subjects. As I read on, I discovered I had made a mistake. Both writers can write about many different subjects.

Section One: I Thought

In her essay "Why I Write", Didion writes she can only write about one subject. Her writing process. Where she gets her ideas, how she forms her characters, etc., Although Dillard likes to write about many different subjects, her favorite subject is being alone. Dillard likes to write about how a mangrove tree is alone.

According to Dillard in her essay "Sojourner", mangrove trees grow on a desert island. The trees grow to be 5 to 6′ tall. They grow in rows 25 to 30′ to the left or right of other trees. The sun constantly beats down on the open mangroves. In order to block out the sun's rays and keep them from beating down on the open mangroves, mangrove trees have to grow to be at least 20 to 30′ tall. They also have to grow side by side, one right after the other encircling one tree. Since mangrove trees don't grow in this way, a mangrove tree must find its own way to beat the heat. Dillard also writes how we are alone.

When Dillard writes about being alone she means, we often have to solve our problems without anyone to help us.

If you have ever lived alone in an apartment in a state where you have no relatives, you understand what Dillard means when she says we are alone.

Because you have no relatives in the state, you have no one to help you if you get into trouble and need help fast.

If you are out of money and your landlord says you have to pay the rent in 24 hours or you will have to find another place to live, you better start looking for another place to live, because there is no one in the state who can lend you the money that fast and it takes at least 2 or 3 weeks to get it from your folks, if you write them a letter asking them for money. Dillard also likes to compare the mangroves feeling of being alone to our feeling of being alone.

In her essay "Sojourner", Dillard writes we are like the mangrove tree, because both of us have to solve our problems without anyone to help us.

When I read this part of Dillard's essay "Sojourner", I thought Dillard was writing about three different subjects. The first subject was how mangrove trees didn't have other mangroves to block out the sun's rays and keep them from beating down on the open mangroves. The second subject was how we often have to solve our problems without anyone to help us. The third subject was her comparison of the mangroves to us. Because I thought Dillard was writing about three different subjects in her essay "Sojourner", I concluded Dillard could write about many different subjects. Since Didion admitted in her essay "Why I Write" she could only write about how she writes, I concluded Didion and Dillard were different writers, because Didion could write about one subject, while Dillard could write about many different subjects.

Section Two: The Teacher Suggested

The day after I had formed this thesis, I had a talk with my teacher. One of the subjects we talked about was my thesis for this essay. When I told her my thesis for this essay she said:

"This is a good thesis, but I'd be careful to balance your evidence when you support your thesis. You can't base the thesis of your essay on one sentence from one of Didion's essays and all of Dillard's essays.

If I were you, I wouldn't take what Didion or Dillard says literally. I've discovered there is a difference between what Didion and Dillard say they write about and what they actually write about. I've discovered from reading Didion's essays, although Didion says she can only write about her writing, she doesn't restrict herself to that subject. She writes about other subjects as well. One of the other subjects she writes about is her personal experiences.

In her essay 'Goodbye to All That', Didion writes about her first trip to New York. Most of the experiences she writes about are situations we can identify with, because we have been in similar situations ourselves. When I asked the class if they could understand what Didion felt when she went to New York for the first time, most of them said they could because most of them have tried something new sometime in their lives, whether it was moving to a new state or changing jobs."

Section Three: The Teacher Was Right

When I got home, I reread Didion's and Dillard's essays. When I reread Didion's and Dillard's essays, I decided the teacher was right. Didion and Dillard are the same writers, because both Didion and Dillard can write about many different subjects. One of the subjects Didion likes to write about is her personal experiences. Didion likes to use her personal experiences to make a point.

When Didion tells us about the time she told one of her friends she could see the Brooklyn bridge from the window of her apartment in New York, which she later found out was a less famous bridge in her essay "Goodbye to All That", she isn't just telling you it for kicks she is trying to make a point. Her point is: Don't believe everything you see.

Whenever you disobey one of your parents rules like: coming home late from a date when you have to get up for school the next day, your mother will scold you for a few minutes, by telling you not to do that again. When she has finished scolding you, she will tell you about a time when she slept 'til noon on a school day after coming home late from a date. When she tells you this story she isn't telling it to you for kicks, just like Didion, she is trying to make a point. Her point is: If you don't come home on time from a date, you won't be able to get up for school the next morning.

In addition to rereading the essays I had to read to write this essay, I also reread the editor's introduction at the beginning of each writer's body of work for both Didion and Dillard. According to the editor's introduction to Didion's body of work, one subject Didion likes to write about is the reasons for her behavior.

When Didion took her trip to New York, she took with her all her ideas about New York. One of the ideas she took with her was, New York was the land of opportunity jobwise. There were plenty of jobs in New York, Didion thought. All she had to do was decide what job she wanted to apply, fill out an application, drop it off at the personnel office of the company she wanted to work for and she would get the job. 30 years later when Didion published her essay "Goodbye to All That", she wondered why she had that idea. This process isn't exclusive to Didion. We've all done things we regret.

Have you ever had a fight with your husband or wife, boyfriend or girlfriend where halfway through the fight you forget what your fighting about, so you start calling each other names? If you have then you know, later on when things have quieted down you wonder why you said those things.

The End of It

Now that I think about it, I think I was wrong when I said Didion and Dillard are different writers, because Didion can write about one subject, while Dillard can write about many different subjects. It seems clear to me from rereading Didion's and Dillard's essays along with the editor's introduction at the beginning of Didion's and Dillard's body of work, Didion and Dillard are the same rather than different writers, because both writers can write about many different subjects.

Appendix 3–2: One Freshman's Adjustment

The transition from high school to college affected my life profoundly. My social life seemed to be the area that changed the most in my transition. There are some specific experiences that portray the adjustment I went through.

I lived in what I now sometimes joke about and sarcastically call dormland or dormville. For my first two semesters, actually, it wasn't so bad. Dormlife is what had actually contributed most to my development of many new, lasting friendships. I also owe my ability to open up and become a lot less shy than I was in my past years to these wonderful living quarters. I would highly encourage and recommend all incoming freshman to live in the dorms for at least their first year to experience the social-life and to develop so many new friends.

Another aspect of the college scene is partying of course. During high school, I thought parties were going out with friends and having a "good time". Well, I guess I just didn't really know what a "good time" was then. The first party I was ever at in college was a frat. party at the frat. house. I was so taken aback at how many people were there. At first I felt shy and hung around only the people who I had come with. I then began thinking, well there are so many people here—I could meet so many new friends here and have even a better time. No, I'm not forgetting the major part of college partying— alcohol. I mostly drank socially at parties. I usually knew my limits and wouldn't try to beat them. There were a few times, but everyone knows how that goes.

Another one of my experiences in college was one that is pretty human and happens to many of us at one time or another. Everyone knows how hard it is to say "no" to something that they really want to do, and "yes" to something they *have* to do. This happened during my first semester of college. I became such a partier and was having so much fun living at college that I got a little bit too involved with the social-scene. I found myself saying "yes" to any and every opportunity to have a good time and go out or party. I thought, well, I'll find time to study later this week or tomorrow when nothing is going on. Well, it turned out, the "later this week" or "tomorrow" wasn't enough time or sometimes never even came. As a result my grades were not as good as I had aimed for and I was falling far behind in my classes. Fortunately, by second semester I learned to balance my time more effectively, and learned how to say no.

In conclusion, my horizons were broadened by college in many ways. My social life had definitely changed for the better. I learned things such as how to open-up and make lots of new and lasting friendships, and to be able to say "no". It was a profound change that occurred over a short period of time. I think this transition helped me with a lot of areas I needed help with. For instance, opening-up helped to get rid of my shyness and saying "no" helped me become a more responsible student. There were a few ups and downs involved, but the adjustment I made turned out to be very successful.

*A*ppendix 3–3: *Collage: 1972*

Before:

Looking up from my Matchbox toy cars, I saw the bodies leaving Vietnam on our T.V., bagged and stacked like trash on the curb. I saw the waves of police and National Guard sweep across the screen, truncheons swinging freely, people crumbling and stumbling under their boots. And the fire hoses, as if the crowd could be doused and extinguished and washed away like dirt off a driveway. I saw the funeral of JFK; the gray and white flag limp over his horse drawn coffin. I heard the slow sonorous singing of the "Battle Hymn of the Republic," saw the tears on the T.V. and my mother. I remember the world in that little box spilling into our home, my uncle sleeping on the floor, for comfort, on the night of King's murder. I turned away from the gray blood and tears on our T.V., and back to the bright yellows and reds of my toy Fords and Fiats.

Pushing these cars across our floor, I had no tears of my own to offer. If I had feelings, they passed without mark, save the later shame of having not known and not cared. Sometimes it's as though I have betrayed my generation, my descendants, my ancestors, by not caring about the bullets and bombs in the world, by running my toy cars up and down the carpet while our black and white Zenith exploded with violence.

During:

When I became a swimmer, I packed away my matchbox cars on basement shelves. My closet needed room for swimsuits, goggles and

stacks of "Swimming World" magazines. By 1972 the magazines had
had dozens of articles about Mark Spitz, and I was anxiously waiting
for him to swim his star-spangled swimsuit to Olympic glory. Seven
times Spitz captured the gold medal, each win was in world record
time, and seven times I watched the red, white and blue flag raised
above his head, my throat knotting and eyes threatening teardrops.
Later at Olympiad, faceless armed men stalked the Olympic Vil-
lage, finding the rooms of some Israeli coaches and athletes. Eleven
of us were murdered that night, and I stayed up all night with Frank
McKay while he showed us maps of the violence and eventually
gunshot flashes in the dark. Eleven fellow athletes were murdered by
that unreal world which could only reach me through that little box
and picture tube. It was as if the terrorists had not only scaled the
walls of their victims' building, but the walls of my home and my
Olympic dreams.

Over Vietnam, Andy Pick was killed. Carl, his older brother and
my swim coach at the time, wore sunglasses to practice that evening.
I never saw his tears, but the water tasted salty. A jealous husband
had planted a bomb in his wife's suitcase, and all aboard were lost as
the plane flew over Vietnam. Andy was a swimmer at the University
of North Carolina; some dreams have time bombs.

At the Wisconsin Junior Olympics that summer, I stood on the
starting platform above the blue fifty-meter field. Before me, long
red and white lane markers narrowed toward the opposite shore.
Sparks of sunlight halted their dance, and for less than a beat the
water was a star-filled daylight sky, gleaming blue and light. The
sound of the crowd vanished, and for that instant of silence and
stillness there was clarity; internal, singular and complete. The earth
had ceased turning to give me a moment to understand. Later,
merged into the blue, there was only the sound of my own heart
beating until I turned my ear to breathe and heard the roar of the
spinning of the earth and saw faces and backs, watching and turning.
Still, my course was clear, the black cross on the finish wall grew
steadily larger and if the world had fallen away, leaving only myself
and the pool, my life would have swum on.

Although I did not win this race, I was in it, had seen the pool and
the finish cross. I had seen the blue and red and white ribbons
embossed with Olympic gold letters and trimming. I brought home
no ribbons, only a dream stolen from Spitz, one he had used and
made real.

After:

All these memories collage now to fill these pages as they did in 1972 to form a universe, a universe of dreams and bombs. A world, distant and unreal, behind television glass, broke into my dreams and life, encasing me like pool water, supporting me, challenging me and sustaining my vigor. I cared in 1972, first about swimming, then the swimming world and finally the world itself. The pain of real life existence somehow reached me.

Swimming was the glue—the images that were cast, stuck. The tears, the bullets, the cross, the flag, the gold, the blue. We learn to care, first for ourselves, but then for others. When we have the glue to hold these images against our memories and hopes, then we are ready to plunge from that starting platform into the blue and light, where we can chase our dreams with complete and utter dedication. We can collage a universe from the images of our past, our present and our future and understand the pain and joy of the race.

4

Teaching like a Reader Instead of Reading like a Teacher

Virginia A. Chappell

If they saw us bent over our desks, colored pen in hand, a stack of typed pages on either side of us, what would our students—or, for that matter, our colleagues in other departments—say we were doing? Grading papers. What most writing teachers consider themselves to be doing in this situation, however, is far more significant and complicated than attempting merely to quantify our multifaceted responses to students' papers, responses we customarily attempt to articulate by writing comments in margins. The complex work that we do bent over these papers is the central task of our profession, central not because grades or even evaluation are crucial to a writer's development, but because response is. Those of us who conceive of writing as a way of knowing can agree with those of us who understand it primarily as means of communicating: learning about someone else's response to a written text is all-important to the writer's own understanding of meanings made and to be made.[1]

One of the primary difficulties we face in responding to student papers is that we are expected to serve many masters. How should we sort out our obligations? What purpose do our responses serve? The institutional necessity for a grade is the bottom line. On our way there we try to make obeisance to ideals of Good Writing and Improvement and to acknowledge the sophistic devils of Fairness. Distracting us further from our task are miscellaneous assortments of rules about usage or, perhaps, departmental controversies about grade inflation. A composition teacher working through a stack of student papers must strike many an awkward pedagogical pose as she or he tries to balance allegiance to students' earnest efforts at expression and communication against her or his own professional sense of effectiveness, convention, and correctness.

It is easy, in this tangled state, to overlook the epistemic significance of response as part of composing. (I use "composing" here as Berthoff does, to name the process through which one makes meaning.) But a reader's response offers a writer crucial indications of meanings made and communicated. My purpose in this essay, as its title suggests, is to explore the ways in which the evolution of composition and reading theories over the past two decades revises traditional notions of what goes on when a writing instructor sits down with a student paper outside the presence of its author. The *teaching like a reader* which I advocate is grounded in the insights of transactional reading theory and epistemic rhetorical theory.

I want to insist that the way we address our responses, even in the margins of students' papers, conveys our assumptions about how written discourse works, about where the authority for making meaning through it lies. We need to recognize that just as the piles of papers we must grade can become the dreaded center of our teaching lives, so too the rhetoric of the conversation that focuses on them is the center of *what* we teach, not merely *how* we teach. In other words, teachers' written comments are not a substitute for something, for oral interaction with the writer or for the cryptic inadequacy of grades themselves. Nor do they provide a model that if imitated will lead to improved grades. Rather, marginal and end comments are a special added feature of school writing: an articulation of response that dramatizes the process of a reader constructing a text. Thus they are a means by which the *student* can judge the success of the paper.

The process movement that arose during the 1970s, urging concentration not on written products but on the composing behaviors that produce them, highlighted the role of teacher response as a means of enhancing students' overall development as writers, as opposed to the more limited goal of improving specific textual performance. Through the 1980s, as researchers and theorists broadened their focus to consider the interaction of composing processes with social context, the role of readers in constructing a text drew increasing attention. In *Constructing Texts,* George Dillon summarizes the new concepts of reading that were developing in literary criticism and psycholinguistics:

> The meaning of the text is not on the page to be extracted by readers; rather, it is what results when they engage (e.g., scan, study, reread) texts for whatever purposes they may have and with whatever knowledge, values, and preoccupations they bring to it. Thus the written marks on the page more resemble a musical score than a computer program; they are marks cuing or prompting an enactment or realization by the reader rather than a code requiring deciphering. (xi)

Teaching like a reader is a matter of foregrounding the processes of reading and writing as processes of meaning construction based on, but not entirely constrained by, text. Teaching like a reader understands that both reading and writing are *composing* activities. Thus, it seeks to develop students' awareness of the intersection of writer and reader through text. Success at this kind of teaching involves considerable revision of the mythology of writing that most of our students—and many of us!—have lugged into our classes.

That mythology includes what I call *reading like a teacher:* the faultfinding summative evaluation of student papers that makes grades, their bestowal and their receipt, so distasteful. Researchers such as Nancy Sommers and Cy Knoblauch and Lil Brannon have pretty thoroughly condemned this kind of response as ineffective, but it flourishes nevertheless. Sommers's research shows that too frequently the primary function, intentional or not, of teachers' written comments has been to justify a grade. Worse, teachers' comments can be counterproductive, for, she says, they "can take students' attention away from their own purposes in writing a particular text and focus that attention on the teachers' purpose in commenting" ("Responding" 149). Furthermore, Sommers's study found that "most teachers' comments are not text-specific and could be interchanged, rubber-stamped, from text to text" (152).

Both ancient and contemporary rhetoricians suggest that a rhetoric will always serve a particular formulation of knowledge or power, and our comments on student papers are no exception. Certainly these comments have a rhetorical aim. Although they perhaps do not directly seek to persuade, they do, in Burke's terms, use language "as a symbolic means of inducing cooperation" (*Rhetoric of Motives* 43).

It follows that as teachers of rhetoric and composition, each of us has a professional obligation to formulate the rhetorical grounds of our comments, to work out the assumptions upon which we will read student writing and upon which we will frame our responses to it for those students: applauding, redirecting, and, yes, measuring their efforts.

Teaching like a reader fits with what Kenneth Dowst has dubbed the "epistemic" approach to composition, which presupposes that writing is "a means of knowing and of coming-to-know" (72) and that language is itself a means of perception. Such an approach, he points out, necessitates giving students opportunities to "manipulate language in ways that enable them to discover for themselves, and in their own terms, what it means to manipulate language" (73). When it is time to sit down with a stack of student papers, an instructor who teaches like a reader takes social and transactional understandings of composing into account and seeks to provide students with commentary that will facilitate the development of the students' own ideas, not just about a paper's content, but about how a particular formulation of those ideas has been read. Fundamentally, then, teaching like a reader turns the student writer outward and presents a broadly contextualized concept of the reciprocal processes of writing and reading texts.[2]

In the classroom itself, teaching like a reader means instituting activities that provide for multiple levels of response to student papers—including teacher-student conferences and peer workshops—at a variety of stages in students' composing processes. However, depending upon how one conceives of and presents the purpose of these activities, their use perhaps ought only be dubbed "teaching like a writer." That is, it is important that students understand the activities as opportunities to gather responses about how readers are constructing their texts, rather than merely as procedures through which good writers are supposed to put themselves.

Rooted in research about composing processes, most contemporary discussions about response to student writing have agreed on the value of comments on preliminary drafts, of writers' hearing how readers perceive their work while it is still provisional, open to change. (This kind of response is known as formative evaluation because, instead of summing up achievement, it treats the text as still in process, still formable.) Pedagogy that emphasizes exercises in response and revision to enhance recursive stages of writing grows out of efforts to replicate the self-monitoring composing processes exhibited by expert writers in compose-aloud studies such as those conducted by Linda Flower and John Hayes. When these activities imitating recursiveness are presented as a model of expert writing behavior, they tell students only what writers—good writers, granted—do, and suggest that imitating the behaviors, acting "like a writer," leads to successful writing. Indeed, it may. However, teaching like a reader pushes beyond "how-to" models of writerly behavior and brings the reader into the picture as a co-composer. Thus, it both reflects and asserts the deepening complexity of contemporary notions of both the writing process and pedagogical response to student writing.

From the perspective of current theoretical work in rhetoric, reading, and poststructuralist literary criticism, response becomes not just a model to be internalized but the crucial event through which written discourse has its effect. Dillon's metaphor of the musical score captures the increasingly central notion that meaning making occurs only through a writer's transaction with a reader. Influenced by a variety of social and political circumstances as well as the tenets of classical rhetoric, specialists in rhetoric and composition have come to emphasize the social and contextual constraints that impinge on both student and professional writing. (James Berlin's "Rhetoric and Ideology" and Lester Faigley's "Competing Theories of Process" provide overviews of the varying theoretical positions.) On the frontiers of rhetorical theory, knowledge is taken to be a function of intersubjectivity. As Berlin puts it, "Communication is at the center of epistemic rhetoric because knowledge is always knowledge for someone standing in relation to others in a linguistically circumscribed situation" (*Rhetoric and Reality* 166).

Notions of subjectivity and intersubjectivity are crucial in the various formulations of reader-response criticism as well. Louise Rosenblatt's notion of *transaction* is perhaps the most relevant for teacher-response issues. Rosenblatt holds that a poem (by which she means any literary work) exists only in the reader-text interaction, during which the reader transforms the text into the poem. A poem is not an object, she says, but an "experience shaped by the reader under the guidance of the text" (12). Although Rosenblatt's theory may posit too individual a literary response and put too little emphasis on intertextuality to suit Berlin, who emphasizes the ideology of his own position as *social*-epistemic ("Rhetoric and Ideology"), the two hold parallel concepts of how written discourse works. The notion of transaction is central for reading theorists, too. Jerome Harste, Vir-

ginia Woodward, and Carolyn Burke, reflecting on their extensive
study of the literacy experiences children have before they reach
school, emphasize the interaction between learner and environment.
The transactional view of language learning they propose "assumes
that meaning resides neither in the environment nor totally in the
head of the language learner, but rather is the result of on-going sign
interpretation" (93).

These transactional assumptions about the nature of reading and
writing are at odds not only with the stereotype of the teacher passing
judgment upon text after text, but with the formalist assumptions
that animate such activity. The *reading like a teacher* from which I
mean to dissuade my own readers is still bound by formalist assumptions that meaning, identical with expression, lies in the text. Such a
view implies that the misunderstandings around which I. A. Richards
defines rhetoric are avoidable. They are not. Indeed, the art of rhetoric
(and its manifestation as composition instruction) is necessitated by
the inevitability of misunderstanding.[3] Edward White, connecting
current composition theory and practice directly to the premises of
poststructuralist literary theory, points out:

> If we are limited to what the student put on the paper,
> we tend to be literalists, putting aside our intuitions of
> what the student meant to say or our predictions of what
> the student *could* say if he or she followed the best insights
> of the text. This formalistic misreading of student writing,
> which pretends to be objective, demands that the student
> believe that *our* concept of what was written is what is
> "really" there. (191)

As Sommers as well as Knoblauch and Brannon have described, such
reading leads teachers to appropriate the student's text by measuring
it against an Ideal Text of the teacher's own conceiving, against
which it is inevitably found wanting. Instead, White and these others
recommend readings that make students "conscious of readers and
of the ways readers interact with their texts" (White 192).

If a writing teacher's engagement with the text is necessarily a
transaction with it, only the sanctions of institutional authority can
transform that response into a judgment upon the text's author. The
way readers usually interact with texts is akin to what Alan Purves
describes as a "common reader" (one of eight potential roles he
sketches for teachers as readers), granting a writer primary textual
authority and reading with good will, "out of pleasure and interest"

(260). But, as we know, teachers tend to read students' texts to evaluate them, and, as William Irmscher has pointed out, teachers tend to evaluate by finding fault (148). In fact, the authority to evaluate and grade exists separately from the act of reading. It has only a secondary, even tangential relationship to the normal process of making meaning.

We return to the original question: what, then, is our commenting for? Which master should it serve, formative or summative evaluation, the writer's ideas or external grading standards?

The answer, of course, must be both, but not necessarily at the same time. It is a mark of good teaching to keep one's obligations to each separate and to communicate this distinction to one's students. Our primary concern must be not with papers but with our students' development as writers. Our real purpose is to enable students to become good readers and good revisers of their own writing. A major factor in this development is learning how to get and use response. We also want our students to become good collaborators, good respondents to other people's writing. Again, the substantive responses they receive are crucial. The grading can wait. Being summative, after all, it belongs at the end. In the meantime, the purpose of our response should be to facilitate the students' efforts to discover and communicate meaning. Transactional reading theory and epistemic rhetoric tell us that it is the give-and-take of dialogue, spoken and written, that teaches students about the effect of their texts, not the excellent advice we can sometimes find ourselves expounding in the margins. Furthermore, it is the give-and-take of this responsive, facilitative dialogue which I contend lies at the core of our professional work, that makes teaching fun. It is here that we teachers, like readers, learn about our students' lives and about the intricate, surprising possibilities of language used (and misused) for purposes that sometimes can go awry but that sometimes can stun us with insight.

Once we set aside (albeit temporarily) the evaluative functions of commenting on student papers, the immediate purpose of teacherly response to student writing is to assist the students with what Berthoff calls an audit of meaning and thus, usually, to motivate and facilitate revision. Sarah Freedman describes the response process as "collaborative problem-solving" (7). But before we move to the problem-solving, we need to establish grounds for the collaboration. We need to remember all the admonitions we have heard about the value of being positive in our responses, because an even more fundamental purpose for response than promoting revision is assuring students that their writing is valuable and important. They need to know that the meaning they are making with their prose engages another person's interest, that it matters. Only out of a sincerely established congruence of goals between teacher/reader and student/writer can the collaboration proceed. These goals will vary from course to course, student to student, paper to paper. Reaching them is a matter of helping students discover and articulate the meaning they want to create and of guiding them to do this in a manner compatible with whatever pragmatic and formal constraints apply.

Implicit in talking this way about student texts and our response to them is a very delicate shift of authority, a relinquishing of the teacher's authority as evaluator complemented by an enhancement of his or her authority as reader. Knoblauch and Brannon point up this trade-off nicely when they say facilitative comments should "preserve the writer's control of the discourse, while also registering uncertainty about what the writer wishes to communicate" (128). They recommend procedures for response that resemble negotiations over meaning, suggesting that the respondent "offer perceptions of uncertainty, incompleteness, unfulfilled promises, unrealized opportunities, as motivation for more writing and therefore more learning about a subject as well as more successful communication of whatever has been learned" (123). Berthoff calls this inquiring stance *interpretive paraphrase,* a dialogue technique focusing on meaning. Her suggestions, like those of Knoblauch and Brannon, leave with the writer any responsibility to correct a reader's misunderstandings. But Berthoff reminds us that the questions should be genuine inquiries, not demands for performance. She suggests, for example, that "'How does it change your meaning if you put it this way?' is more likely to engender critical thinking on the students' part than, 'What do you mean?'" (*Making of Meaning* 115). Another technique that helps students focus their thinking is to ask what would happen to the meaning if a troublesome section of text were simply left out. The search for an answer often reveals the gist of what the writer was struggling to articulate.[4]

This role of teacher as "reader attempting to understand the text" is, as Robert Probst points out, the model of the reader's role put forward by transactional reading theory (70). Ironically, the attribution of authority in transactional announcements, such as Constance Weaver's statement that "what the reader brings to the text is crucial in determining the meaning," may come as no surprise to cynical students who have complained all along about biased grades or tried unsuccessfully to figure out "what the teacher wants." However, the real paradox of transactional theory's contribution to response pedagogy is the way that the description of a more active role for readers entails lessening the authority of the teacher *qua* teacher over a text. No longer are meaning or textual efficacy considered to be measurable from an external objectivity, an objectivity to which teachers are more privy than students. Instead, a teacher comes to a student text with respect, seeking more to understand than to evaluate. Probst describes the encounter as a "shared commitment" to the pursuit of meaning (70). His assertion of "commitment" is crucial, for without the mutual pursuit of meaning we might be caught in a situation of warring subjectivities, of competing Rorschach interpretations.

It is exactly this new understanding of the negotiability and tentativeness of textual meanings that may be the most difficult concept of all to teach. As Michael Reddy has shown, the notion of language as a conduit and of meaning as something that can be packaged, transmitted, and received through it is rooted deeply in our language about language. In Frank Smith's powerful contrast of metaphors, the formalist assumptions of what I have dubbed "reading like a teacher" treat communication as a shunting of information, "the exchanging of messages like sums of money or bags of oranges" (195). He proposes instead that we think of literacy as the creation of interpersonal worlds:

> Thought in its broadest sense is the construction of worlds, both "real" and imaginary, learning is their elaboration and modification, and language—especially written language—is a particularly efficacious but by no means unique medium by which these worlds can be manifested, manipulated, and sometimes shared. (197)

Martin Nystrand's emphasis on *reciprocity* in the writing and reading of texts helps suggest the new kind of interactions we might have with and encourage among our students to promote a transactional viewpoint that not only is receptive to our readerly teaching but also fosters readerly responses from students. (See Nystrand and Brandt's research on peer response.) In his formulation of "A Social-Interactive Model of Writing," which is congruent with the transactional models of reading discussed here, Nystrand asserts that "texts have meaning not to the extent that they represent the writer's purpose but rather to the extent that their potential for meaning is realized by the reader" (76). Like Harste and his colleagues, Nystrand discards both a formalist position that would fix meaning in the text and an idealist position that would accept assertions of meaning from multiple subjectivities. He argues that *"meaning is between writer and reader"* (78; his emphasis). Nystrand describes written communication as "a fiduciary act" and says that a writer connects to a reader's world by "elaborating text in accord with what the writer can reasonably assume that the reader knows and expects," and that a reader collaborates in the process by "predicting text in accord with what the reader assumes about the writer's purpose" (75). Invoking a phrase from Ragmar Rommetveit, Nystrand says that "as long as writers write on the premises of readers and readers read on the premises of writers, the result is coherent communication" ("Reciprocity" 41; Rommetveit 63).

One of the very important functions of teacher response to student writing is helping students learn to write on the premises of readers. (This function explains why peer response is so valuable as well.) Very often our puzzled responses help students transform writer-based prose into reader-based prose in exactly Linda Flower's terms. Beyond this practical benefit, the premises of contemporary reading theory and poststructuralist literary criticism suggest the advantages of teaching about the dynamics of reading, about readers' premises. The mythologies of objective observation and transparent texts have kept the majority of students in composition classes from discovering the subtleties either of reading on the premises of writers or of writing on the premises of readers. Students have read many textbooks and learned to read on the premises of gleaning information. They have learned to write on the premises of performing for the teacher. Collaboration and reciprocity are missing from this picture.

But providing for these interactions is not the whole story of teaching like a reader. Teachers need to read on the premises of *student* writers. Combining different kinds of response activities is a delicate act to perform, for we are not, after all, merely "common readers." We have obligations to help students with discovery and with conventions, to guide them toward improved texts and enhanced awareness of composing processes, to show them how writers write and readers read. And we are obliged to do all this without usurping the students' own textual authority, without appropriating even predictable or truncated texts into much more interesting ones of our own. We can teach students to write on the premises of readers by reading their work on the premises of *developing* writers. That is, since we do have more experience as writers and readers than they do, and since we do know more about rhetorical and stylistic techniques that make for effective prose, we have specific expertise to offer through our comments. Teaching like a reader involves a doubling of our readerly consciousness: a facilitative reading that looks beyond an awareness of textual product to become aware of and inquire about meaning-rich process.

The techniques of error analysis, developed by second language acquisition researchers in the mid-1970s, provide an analogous method of reading. The assumption behind error analysis is that grammatical errors offer certain kinds of readers—teachers and re-searchers—valuable information because these errors often reflect a systematic but idiosyncratic grammar and thus can reveal acquisition strategies (see Kroll and Shafer's summary).[5] Implicit here is the transactional concept of meaning-making dialogue between reader and writer. Mina Shaughnessy's method in *Errors and Expectations* was informed by the error analysis notion that if one misreads the literal surface text to infer intention, one may uncover complex linguistic hypotheses that, when recognized and modified, may lead to ever closer approximations of appropriate linguistic forms.

David Bartholomae expands Shaughnessy's approach to incorporate direct consultation with students ("The Study of Error"). He stresses the need for extratextual information from the writer so that the teacher can understand intention and so help the writer solve problems by revising what may have previously been only tacit strategies. This consultation is parallel to that involved in interpretive paraphrase. Leonard and Joanne Podis explicitly draw the analogy of error analysis to the level of rhetorical intention, suggesting that rhetorical weaknesses may represent developmental strivings that have fallen less short of the mark than may appear on the surface. They suggest that instructors "approach draft difficulties as potential keys to understanding student writers' intentions, and in some cases as keys to helping the writers better define their intention in their own minds" (91). These methods suggest important ways in which writing instructors can read on the premises of writers, granting students valuable textual authority over not only their felicitous efforts, but their infelicities as well.

The recommendations of these composition teachers fit with the analyses of the reading and literary theorists. Anthony Petrosky provides a good summary:

> When we read, we comprehend by putting together impressions of the text with our personal, cultural, and contextual models of reality. When we write, we compose by making meaning from available information, our personal knowledge, and the cultural and contextual frames we happen to find ourselves in. Our theoretical understandings of these processes are converging . . . around the central role of human understanding—be it of texts or the world—as a process of composing.[6] (26)

What this convergence of theories tells us about teaching writing *like a reader,* and about responding to student papers in particular, is that the decisions we make about response are not merely methodological.

The rhetoric of our responding posture itself enacts our epistemological assumptions about how written discourse makes meaning. No matter how much we talk in class about "the composing process," if we treat student papers as documents that channel meaning onto our desks for judgment, like tea into a tea-taster's cup, the response process will confirm what most people think written discourse is: a one-way conduit for meaning. If we treat them as tentative explorations that *make meaning* through a transactional process of which our reading is a crucial part, this process has the potential for reshaping our students' understanding of the nature of written discourse while and because it aids their development as writers and readers. We must remember, too, that the texts of our comments function in the same transactional fashion, achieving meaning only when the interaction with a reader is complete. (There is perhaps an extra spin of tentativeness in these transactions, deriving from the students' past experiences of having their texts read by evaluating teachers.) It would be a mistake to think that because we speak from a position of institutional authority, our literally marginal texts *are* capable of shunting information about what is good and bad about a paper. Our scribbles, like other texts, can only be offered for transaction and are open to meaning negotiation. Furthermore, we can expect writing them to be a discovery process, not a transcription of inspiration. (This is why many teachers use pencils for their comments, or pound out a complex but instantaneously erasable response on the computer before deciding what to note later, gracefully, on the student's page.) In a classroom presided over by someone teaching like a reader, even that grade on the bottom line can be understood as part of an ongoing conversation about effectiveness and development.

Transactional theory teaches us that our responses to student writing are more than a model of response that students can internalize to a self-sufficiency. As Harste and his colleagues contend, "Language is not acquired through modeling; it is learned through interpretation" (94). We learn about writing well in large part by interpreting the responses we get. The interaction between teachers and students teaches in two ways. First, it helps students make decisions about their texts: to discover what they want to say, and then assess whether they have said it as they want to, to get the response they want. Second, the interaction dramatizes how meaning resides between the reader and the text. Dillon says that "the writer's fundamental need is the ability to project the experience of readers so that he or she can judge how much to say and how to say it" (164). Our responses to our students' writing are less a model for imitation and more a trying out of their texts. Response allows them to judge how well they have projected their readers' experience. Martin Nystrand, Anne Doyle, and Margaret Himley say that "a text is meaningful not when *what is said* matches *what is meant* but rather when *what is said* strikes a balance between *what needs to be said* and *what may be assumed*" (92–93). Where does one learn such balance? From response. One can get better and better at projecting, but one does not get to a point where one does not need responders. Response is what it is, a moment which dramatizes the making of meaning. In its own fullness and complexity, it is not a substitute for something else. *Teaching like a reader* permits us to experiment with and revel in its pains and its pleasures.

Notes

1. The interlocutor may, of course, be the writer's own self, later or synchronously, as auditor of meaning (Ann Berthoff's phrase) or as seeker of information jotted down for later use.

2. Although my essay focuses on the problem of finding theoretical grounding for teachers' written comments, I want to note that I have much faith in the value of writing groups, individual conferencing, and writing centers. I leave it to my readers to draw appropriate analogies to other genres of response from the theories and tech-

66	Virginia A. Chappell

niques discussed here. For a wealth of resources and ideas for many different sources and modes of response, see Knoblauch and Brannon's book, the bibliographic essay by Brooke Horvath, the essay collection edited by Chris Anson, and the textbooks by Peter Elbow and Pat Belanoff.

3. Richards urged that rhetoric be understood as "a study of misunderstandings and its remedies" (3).

4. Ronald Lunsford and Richard Straub's forthcoming study of composition teachers' various styles of responding to student writing includes a rubric for analyzing the orientation, focus, and mode of comments.

5. As Joseph Williams has shown, errors can also be invisible if readers do not expect to find them.

6. Bruce Petersen's collection of essays on reading and writing theory takes its title from this notion of converging understandings.

5

Talking about Writing and Writing about Talking: Pragmatics in the Composition Classroom

Kathleen Doty

In the field of linguistics today, there is a great deal of talk about talking. This is a significant shift from that recent period when those who contemplated linguistics had in mind the discrete units of linguistic analysis—phonemes, morphemes, grammatical categories— or the larger theoretical paradigms: Saussure's structuralism, for instance, or Chomsky's generative-transformational grammar or Halliday's functionalism. For many, linguistics was the abstract analysis of language segments, whether sounds, words, or sentences. But current linguistic theory now includes a pragmatic component. Defined simply, *pragmatics* is the study of the use and meaning of utterances in context. It includes the study of speech acts, conversational analysis, and discourse analysis. Although research in pragmatics draws from a variety of disciplines, from linguistics to philosophy to anthropology to sociology, the common concern is with utterances beyond the sentence level.

As a result of this focus beyond the sentence level, this interest in talk among individuals, pragmatics moves the student toward the study of utterances and their production, their context, and their meaning and interpretation. Moving beyond the sentence allows both linguists and writing professionals to approach language as communicative action rather than as an autonomous abstract system. Pragmatics views language as multifunctional, as a way of creating the world and acting in it, not simply as a way of reflecting it. It is in these respects that pragmatics shares common ground with current social-epistemic rhetorical theory. Our current interest in the social contexts of writing and the relationships between writer, reader, and text is well served by a pragmatic approach to language study.

With its emphasis on human communication and interaction, pragmatics offers a thoroughly rhetorical model of language and intersects with rhetorical theory and writing instruction in interesting ways. Pragmatics can help explain James Berlin's central point about social-epistemic rhetoric: that knowledge is linguistically conditioned and cannot be divorced from speakers, hearers, and reality (*Rhetoric and Reality* 166). In addition, pragmatics can help meet one important goal of the composition class—to understand the social dynamics of making meaning—by presenting techniques and tools for analysis of language in social contexts. At its best, pragmatics can help students realize some of the theoretical points we try to communicate through assignment and discussion.

A number of recent articles address the relationship between pragmatics and rhetoric, some emphasizing pedagogical applications. For instance, Martin Nystrand's "Social-Interactive Model of Writing" depends upon a pragmatic, discourse-based view of language. In "Rhetoric's 'Audience' and Linguistics' 'Speech Community,'" Nystrand argues that the two disciplines' notions of the roles of readers/hearers/interlocutors raise important critical questions about the nature of writing. While rhetoric's *audience* begins with the writer and moves outward toward the audience, the linguistic notion of a *speech community* begins with the group and moves in toward the individual. These two directions of movement together move us, as scholars and researchers, toward a social perspective on writing: a written text is a social device, written by an individual, for gaining "mutual understandings among members of particular speech communities" (24). "Context as Vehicle: Implicatures in Writing" by Marilyn Cooper and "Speech Act Theory and Writing" by Martin Steinmann, Jr., suggest pedagogical techniques for incorporating pragmatic insights into a writing course. In "J. L. Austin and the Articulation of a New Rhetoric," Reed Way Dasenbrock echoes Berlin when he examines how speech act theory complements the current rhetorical position that "we make—not simply reflect—our world through language" (297).

My concern, like Cooper's and Steinmann's, is to bring pragmatics into the writing classroom in a concrete manner. My basic premise is that the study of spoken conversation can lead to understanding writing from a social perspective. This essay will describe a writing assignment I have created which incorporates the pragmatic analysis of conversation. The assignment helps students realize that the spoken language they use every day and the written language they read and write are vitally connected: both are social, meaning-making activities. I designed the assignment for a freshman English course in which the reading material is primarily fiction, drama, and poetry. The assignment revolves around a transcription of a casual conversation among four adults.[1] The transcribed conversation is reproduced below in appendix 5-1.

The context of the conversation is a musical concert in a small midwestern town; the speakers are four adults: Vickie, Reuben, Cub, and Helen. Vickie and Reuben are a married couple in their middle thirties; Cub, Reuben's younger sister, is in her early twenties; and Helen is the mother of Reuben and Cub. After the group has been seated in the auditorium, they cannot locate their ticket stubs, which they want to retain for a raffle drawing to be held during intermission. The focus of the conversation is thus on locating the tickets, and the conversation's overall shape is goal-directed. It serves as a highly structured piece of discourse with its focused topic, lexical repetition, and array of different speech acts.

As the conversation shows, verbal behavior is governed by a broad range of factors including social situation, interpersonal relations between the participants, and the beliefs and intentions of the participants. The linguistic pragmatician has the enormous job of explaining how it is that we communicate effectively by skillfully bringing together appropriate surface forms, knowledge of interpersonal speech functions, and social contexts. In the case of this conversation, a pragmatic analysis could focus on any number of features: structural cohesion, lexical repetition, turn taking, interruptions and overlaps, or the relationship between the surface speech forms and their interpersonal intentions and effects. These possibilities indicate the range of pragmatic analysis and the complexity of ordinary verbal interaction and its description.

More particularly, this conversation offers students instructive examples of two well-known frameworks for pragmatic description, speech act theory and conversational analysis. Speech act theory treats verbal utterances as acts which are always performed in a specific

context and with specific speakers and hearers. J. L. Austin's classic
How to Do Things with Words was the first presentation of a theory
of language as action. It provides, for example, an explanation for
the multiplicity of verbal acts in line eighteen when Cub says to
Vickie, "You lost the ti:::cket stubs?" An Austinian analysis posits
that in addition to being a grammatical sentence about the ticket
stubs to Vickie, the utterance is both a statement of Cub's belief
that Vickie lost the stubs and an accusation and indication of her
frustration with Vickie. As the example shows, language, situation,
and meaning are inseparable—one of the essential insights of speech
act theory.

Other theorists have extended Austin's proposals, notably John
Searle in *Speech Acts*. Searle sought to systematize Austin's insights
and provide formal explication of the appropriateness conditions for
successfully performing a speech act. He also accounted for a large
and important proportion of speech acts—those which are performed
indirectly. To use line eighteen again, we can see that Cub's utterance
is an indirect speech act. The indirection is conveyed by both grammatical form and the rising intonation which suggests disbelief and/
or frustration with Vickie.

Like Searle, H. Paul Grice is interested in how speakers convey
more than the sense and reference of the spoken locutionary act.
Grice's theory of conversation, as outlined in "Logic and Conversation," posits that a *cooperative principle* (CP) is at work when people
communicate with each other. This principle accounts for indirect
communication since the CP states that people asssume that participants usually intend to communicate effectively within a given context. Under this principle, Grice presents four categories with specific
maxims: Quantity, Quality, Relation, and Manner (45–47). If a
speaker purposively violates any of the maxims during a conversation,
a *conversational implicature* is produced. The hearer assumes that the
CP is in effect and works out what has been implied. For example,
if during a storm at sea I say, "Great day for a boat ride," my hearer
will assume that I am trying to communicate something relevant; the
obvious inference in the situation is that by saying what I believe to
be false, I am conversationally implicating the opposite—that it is a
bad day to be at sea. Similarly, in another example from the conversation (line thirty-eight), Reuben says to Vickie, "Oh very good, Vickie,
you didn't get them back." Given the context of the conversation and
the preceding focus on the lost ticket stubs, we assume Reuben
doesn't actually believe that it is good that Vickie didn't get the stubs;

instead, Reuben conversationally implicates something else, and the most reasonable implicature we can gather is that he means the opposite. But Reuben has not actually said that losing the tickets is bad or that he is unhappy with or disappointed in Vickie. Grice's point is not that we slavishly adhere to conversational maxims, always uttering the truthful and the relevant and providing just the right amount of information. Instead, he suggests that when we purposefully flout maxims our interlocutors will interpret what we are saying as cooperative behavior; they will try to work out the implicature. Grice's work explicates the inferential mechanisms at work in ordinary conversation, and he was one of the first to try to explain how they might fit with standard theories of meaning.

When working with the conversation and these pragmatic principles in the freshman course, I begin by spending a class period discussing the differences between written and spoken language; I gather personal opinions about conversations as well. All students know how to carry on a conversation, but they sometimes need direction in articulating the basic features of spoken talk and how they relate to speakers and participants.[2] For instance, the variation among simple conversational openings such as "good evening," "hello," "hey there," and "what's happenin'" suggests different relationships between speakers or differences in social context. After these discussions, I distribute the conversation, explain the transcription symbols, describe the participants in the conversation, and explain the context.

For most students, it is the first time they have seen a conversation transcribed and put to paper. They are inevitably surprised by its elliptical and fragmented nature, and because of that some students make negative judgments about the participants. Such judgments connect to the discussions we have had about spoken language and how individuals are often stereotyped on the basis of their speech. We discuss the features of spoken language which are not fully captured in transcription (intonation and kinesics, for instance) and how they may affect understanding. I do not tell my students what any particular utterance may have meant in the conversation; rather, I ask them to consider the range of potential meanings the utterances carry. This leads us to discussion of meaning and interpretation, topics we have grappled with throughout the semester as we have read both literature and student essays.

After our discussions, the students are ready to begin the assignment, which is to write three versions of the conversation: first, a short story which includes dialogue from the conversation; second, a dramatic dialogue envisioned as a scene from a play; and third, an expository prose paragraph describing what happens in the conversation. My choice of these forms is linked to the genres we have been reading during the semester, and they provide the students a chance to experiment with new ways of making meaning in writing.

When the students read the conversation, they have little difficulty following it. All indicate that they understand what happens. Yet when they create their versions, they give what happens additional meaning. They draw on their own knowledge of human interaction, interpersonal relations, and motivation to flesh out the conversation. In short, they interpret the participants' actions and utterances. Without direction from me, but drawing on their linguistic and literary competency, they create entertaining stories and dramatic scenes. They make the shift from spoken utterance to written text with an ease and expressiveness that I have not often seen in their previous writings.

Grice claims that the inferential abilities of individuals are evident in conversational interaction, though the inferential mechanisms they use may be unknown to the participants. This ability is at work when one reads as well; the students are able to read the conversation used for this exercise and make correct inferences about the participants and their relationship. One example is in line thirty, where students interpret Reuben's utterances—"I didn't lose them. Where are they? I don't know"—as a mockery and accusation of Vickie. This inference is accurate (as the participants have verified to me), but more importantly it shows that the students are carefully noting the preceding lines and exchanges (especially lines twenty-six, twenty-seven, and twenty-eight). On the basis of the words, the participants, and the context, students are able to retrieve the implicature in Reuben's utterances much as Grice's theory predicts.[3]

The stories and dramatic dialogues are usually the best versions for students because these pieces reflect careful thinking about both literary genre and writing to communicate. For example, one student created a story entitled "The Case of Vickie and the Ticket Stubs," a clever parody of hard-boiled detective stories told from the perspective of the detective. Another student created a first-person narrative by Reuben, while a number of students wrote stories sympathetic to Vickie's position, using various narrative points of view. All students, however, make explicit the motivation for searching for the tickets, and most of them expand upon the interaction between the four people, often using stock characters such as the downtrodden wife, the bored or abusive husband, the quiet, submissive mother-in-law, and the cunning or flirtatious younger sister. The dramatic dialogues likewise make good use of theatrical conventions and characterization. One student presented Vickie as obsessed with contests and games of chance in order to create her character and provide motivation for the excitement and worry about the lost stubs. Another student highlighted the marital relations of Vickie and Reuben and used the possibility of winning the prize (money) as Vickie's hope for leaving Reuben. A third student devised a scene using a sophisticated blend of dialogue, stop action, and an opening soliloquy by Vickie. Again, the results show students' ability to interpret human action and motivation while giving meaning and fullness to their writing.

In contrast to the stories and dramas, students report that the expository paragraph is the most difficult to write, and indeed the paragraphs are not as polished as the stories and dialogues. Students have told me that the paragraphs seem to be "useless" and "a waste of time." Few can imagine a reason for anyone to want to read an expository paragraph describing what happened to the participants. Students have reported that they enjoyed writing the stories and dialogues and that they felt free to do what they wanted, to experiment, and to be creative. In the expository paragraphs, though, they said they felt that they had to "get it right" and that they had to be accurate.

The students' emphasis on "getting it right" brings to mind David Olson's formalist position that for written discourse, the "meaning is in the text" (277). The students seem to experience meaning as text-based when writing exposition more than they do when writing stories and dialogues, where a sense of the shared intentions of writer and reader is more evident. Writing expository prose is tainted for students with institutional strictures of performing, being graded, and getting it right. Rather than working with content and form in a way described by William Irmscher as "a process of discovery" (95), students write their expository paragraphs with an external sense of structure. What Irmscher calls "the shape of content" (95) is not discovered through writing but seen as predetermined, though I do not give them requirements for the expository paragraph. It may be that students give up internalized ideas of the nature of expository prose less easily than they give up ideas about literary genre. We might consider giving more emphasis to the variety of expository forms much as we try to give students a sense of the breadth of literary forms. This assignment asks students to question the notion of text-based meaning and to begin to see how writing is making meaning, not simply expressing the single correct meaning. But many students have problems creating a legitimate context for the expository prose; they cannot envision a purpose for writing the paragraph or an audience for it.

Despite the students' difficulty establishing reciprocity between themselves and their readers in expository prose, the assignment as a whole does draw on their intuitive knowledge of oral language and conversation. When students talk to others casually or read conversations, they are adept at understanding indirection and inference. The assignment makes explicit this pragmatic knowledge and then shows how it works in writing and reading. The students are able to incorporate ordinary features of indirection and inference in the stories and dramatic scenes, but are less able to do it in expository prose. Their successes stem in part from the relationship between oral conversation and dialogue in fiction and drama, while their difficulties owe something to the less obvious relationship between oral conversation and expository prose. I suggest that their failures with expository prose also arise from an inability to make inferences about their readers' thoughts, beliefs, and knowledge *when they are writing in that form.* They are better able to take a social perspective—to cope with the demands of the rhetorical situation and their intended readers—when writing short stories and dramatic scenes.

I also suggest that their successes with stories and dramatic scenes result from being readers of these genres throughout the semester. They are better equipped to write with this kind of reader in mind, since they have been these readers for months. By the final few weeks of the semester when they finish the assignment, the students know better how to carry on a conversation with projected readers of stories and dialogues than with readers of expository prose.

The assignment works particularly well in a literature-based composition course since it simultaneously educates students about the processes of reading and writing. However, a course based on readings in nonfiction can have positive results as well. The key issue for students remains one of learning how to read both expository prose and literature as a conversation between writer and reader, as a negotiation of meaning between writer and reader, and then to learn to write such prose for the reader. Exercises such as mine which are informed by the pragmatic study of language can be an important aid for students as they struggle to create reader-based prose. The knowledge that helps students write stories and dramatic dialogues—knowledge about literary genres and conventions, intuitive knowledge of oral language, and the process of reading literature—has implications for reading and writing expository prose. First, we should work to show students the relationship between literary genres and conventions and expository prose. This can range from the simple identification of genres and techniques (imagery, metaphor, pacing, suspense, and so forth) to more complex analyses of contemporary essayists such as Joan Didion, Gretel Ehrlich, and John McPhee. We should strive to increase students' "expository competence" by making explicit how oral language features such as indirection and implication function in expository prose. Further work in the pragmatic analysis of oral conversation is one way to get at this. Indeed, the assignment I have presented can be modified in a number of ways. It may be instructive, for instance, to vary the context and topic of a recorded conversation to discover if students find different genres easier to compose. One might record conversations by businesspeople, politicians, political activists, educators, and so on, and again ask students to create different versions of these conversations in different genres.

The results of this assignment are useful for the rhetorician interested in making concrete for students Berlin's view of knowledge as the dialectical interaction of observer, discourse community, and material conditions. For example, most students created discourses which were grounded in what they perceived to be the economic realities of the participants. They emphasized the possibility of winning money, and often the need for money was linked to the character's personality and situation. Thus, the unhappy wife, Vickie, wanted to flee her marriage; her dream was to live independently on the large sum of money won at the concert. The projected readers are those who accept the legitimacy of a chance winning of money to improve the conditions of one's life. (The emphasis on winning money is particularly revealing since the prize that the real-life participants had a chance to win was never specified.) In another student's discourse, the unhappy wife remembers fondly her old boyfriend, who is a featured musician at the concert. The story ends with the concert beginning, the missing tickets found but the prize not won, and the wife resigned to the patronizing behavior of her husband.

What the students know about the participants and the context has been learned from language only, and what they then create is also expressed solely through language. Language as a social phenomenon, one that contains ideological notions about economics, social, and political arrangements, is well presented in the students' discourses. Working with students to unpack these ideological positions from the discourses they have created is an added benefit of the exercise.

The assignment presented here shifts the emphasis from the discourse features and structures on which traditional pragmatic analysis focuses to the relationship among different forms of language use and between meaning and interpretation. It asks students to work with their own interpretive abilities and to consider the social, communicative nature of spoken and written language. By studying an ordinary conversation and writing different versions of it, students come to see how writing, like spoken conversation, is a social, meaning-making activity. They are also better able to understand the transactional nature of writing by considering the transactional nature of verbal interaction. Through this assignment, the students can experience the theoretical points we want to make about language and writing as social human activities.

As a linguist teaching composition and literature as well as linguistics, I want to encourage a balance of the study of language and the teaching of writing. Pragmatics-based assignments are one way to accomplish this balance. Pragmatics can enrich the rhetoric of writers through its detailed explanations of utterances in context, context-dependent strategies and forms, and general principles of interpretation such as Grice's cooperative principle. Learning how spoken language works and understanding the interpretive strategies used by speakers and hearers in casual, ordinary conversations can help our students in their attempts to make and remake the world through language.

Notes

1. My description of the assignment is for a freshman English course; the conversation, however, was recorded and transcribed by a student in my introductory linguistics course at the University of Wisconsin–Whitewater. I thank the student who gave me permission to use her conversation in the assignment and to publish it here.

2. What students know about conversation and how they experience face-to-face verbal interaction, however, will vary according to their background. My sample is relatively homogeneous, reflecting the white, middle-class status of the participants and the students. In a more multicultural classroom, the discussion about spoken conversation may be different since the natural language environment of students influences conceptions of both face-to-face conversation and verbal interaction in the classroom. Terry Dean's recent article in *CCC* discusses the problems students and instructors face in multicultural writing classrooms. Shirley Brice Heath's *Ways with Words* eloquently chronicles the differences in language development between children in black and white working-class communities.

3. By examining conversations and inferential strategies, Grice considers more than one utterance in sequence. Thus, his work is often included in the field of discourse analysis, the study of utterances longer than one sentence. Generally, discourse analysis strives to characterize speaker (or writer) meaning and to explain it in context of use. Discourse analysis also tries to account for coherence and sequential organization in discourses. Exactly how this is done varies greatly and draws on research in philosophy, psychology, anthropology, sociology, speech communication, and linguistics. As a result of this diversity, there is little consensus about what constitutes discourse analysis, and often the work of individuals in different academic disciplines is grouped together because the insights dovetail and elucidate each other. A sampling of the wide range of topics would include the study of links between one sentence and the next (as in cohesion studies by Halliday and Hasan and others following them); the ethnology of speech; and the study of speech events and speech genres such as interviews, sermons, public speeches, letters, as well as conversations and their structure (represented in the work of Gumperz and Hymes, Hymes, Labov and Fanshel, Tannen, and many others). For a complete and readable introduction to the area, see Malcolm Coulthard, *An Introduction to Discourse Analysis*.

Appendix 5–1: Transcript of Conversation

Transcribing Conventions

The transcription symbols used in the following transcribed conversation are based on the work of Schenkein and others.

Example of Symbol	*Explanation*
A: I don't [think] B: [You] don't	Brackets indicate that the portions of utterances in brackets occurred simultaneously.
A: We:::ll now	Colons indicate that the immediately prior syllable is prolonged.
CAPS or *italics*	Both of these represent heavier emphasis (in speaker's pitch) on the words so marked.
A: That's what I said= B: =But you didn't	Equal signs indicate that no time elapses between the words "latched" by the marks. It often means that the next speaker starts at precisely the end of the current speaker's utterance.
(2.5)	Numbers in parentheses indicate the seconds and tenths of

	seconds ensuing between speaker turns.
(#)	Pound sign indicates a pause of about a second.
(word)	Words in single parentheses indicate that something was heard but the transcriber is not sure what it was.
((softly))	Double parentheses enclose "descriptions," not transcribed utterances.
A: I (x) I did	An *x* in parentheses indicates a hitch or stutter of the speaker.
A: Oh Yeah?	Punctuation marks are used for intonation, not grammar.
.hh hh heh-heh	These are breathing and laughing indicators. A period followed by "hh" marks an inhalation. The "hh" alone stands for exhalation. The "hehs" are laughter syllables.

Conversation

1. Vickie: Did you get a program?
2. Helen: Did you have (x) [Did you get the stubs?]
3. Reuben: [Nobody gave *me* a]
   [program.]
4. Cub: What?
5. Vickie: I hope I do.
6. Reuben: I hope I have a stub.
7. Cub: What?
8. Reuben: A stub.
9. Vickie: They're probably in my coat pocket.
10. Reuben: I don't know why=
11. Vickie: =I've got all four stubs. Will you hang on to that for a second please? ((Hands the tape recorder to Reuben))
12. Cub: Are we recording here now too?

13. Vickie: ⌈I've got to make⌉ every second count.
              ⌊   ⌋ ((Begins to search
                                    through coat
                                    pockets))
14. Reuben: ⌊Well I don't know⌋
15. Reuben: Now what are you doing? (1.0) Getting
             out your JuJuBees?
16. Vickie: No. I'm looking for the ticket stubs.
17. Reuben: Your ah (#) ⌈What do they call those⌉
                          ⌊things you get=   ⌋
18. Cub: ⌊You lost the ti:::cket stubs?⌋
19. Reuben: =from the store? Jaw breakers.
20. Vickie: They must be in my purse. (10.0)
             ((Searches through purse))
21. Cub: With any luck, no one will pick ours. (2.0)
22. Reuben: Come on, Vickie. You kiddin' me.
23. Helen: (words)
24. Cub: She lost them ⌈already.   ⌉
25. Reuben: ⌊She lost them.⌋
26. Vickie: No I didn't.
27. Reuben: Well, where are they then?
28. Vickie: I don't know.
29. Cub: heh-heh
30. Reuben: I didn't lose them. Where are they? I don't
             know.
31. Vickie: Well how could I have lost them? I had
             them in my hand. ((Begins to look through
             purse again))
32. Cub: They have to be in your=
33. Vickie: =I forgot to pu(x) put the bills in the mail.
             ((Pulls several envelopes from purse))
34. Reuben: heh-heh
35. Vickie: I worked on them all day today and then I
             bring them with me.
36. Reuben: You probably handed them to that man
             and then he (#) thank you (#) and then
             walked away.
37. Vickie: .hh He's got 'em! He had them to find out
             where we were seated.

38. Reuben: Oh very good, Vickie, you didn't get them back.
39. Vickie: Is that him? ((refers to usher))
40. Reuben: That's him. Ya better ask him. (6.0) Are you sure he didn't give you back your tickets?
41. Cub: I don't believe this. heh-heh
42. Reuben: You'd better ask him. (2.0) He didn't give me any. I didn't have any tickets. (6.0)
43. Vickie: I'll check my coat pockets. (3.0) Is he the same usher?=
44. Reuben: =Yes, the same usher. (2.0) Way to go, Vickie.
45. Vickie: ((standing)) We'll never get them back.
46. Cub: Do you want to get out? (4.0)
47. Reuben: This is (#) I don't believe this.
48. Helen: Are you sure she gave them to you?
49. Reuben: *He* had them (#) according to her. Now *they're* coming in. ((more people are coming in to be seated)) You'd better just get his attention.
50. Cub: Excuse me. (5.0)
51. Reuben: Did ya=
52. Vickie: =Excuse me. Did you give us back our ticket stubs?
53. Usher: I don't have them. (words) (3.0)
54. Cub: heh-heh
55. Vickie: Well, I've gone through my pockets already.
56. Reuben: I'm hanging on to this stuff.
57. Usher: I gave them to=
58. Cub: =I got 'em! heh-heh
59. Reuben: heh-heh
60. Usher: That's all right=
61. Vickie: =Thank you=
62. Usher: =I don't have any extras.
63. Cub: heh-heh
64. Vickie: Well at least *I'm* vindicated.
65. Reuben: heh-heh

66. Cub: heh-heh. Thank you very much. heh-heh.
              ⎡Here Vickie. Hold them.⎤
67. Vickie: ⎣I (x) I did not lose them.⎦
68. Reuben: heh-heh. Now Vickie's got 'em. Remem-
              ber that=
69. Vickie: =Okay=
70. Reuben: =and keep track of these things.
71. Vickie: Now I will put them in the zipper compart-
              ment. ((puts the ticket stubs into purse))
72. Reuben: Oh, jeez.
73. Vickie: ((to Helen)) Did you hear the bad time
              my husband was giving me because he
              thought I was being irresponsible?
74. Reuben: How did we ever get such good seats?
75. Vickie: I never even had them.
76. Cub: (words) heh-heh
77. Vickie: What?
78. Cub: Bill's seats.
79. Reuben: That's why they are good seats.
80. Vickie: Oh (#) yeah.

6

*M*utual Friends: What Teachers Can Learn from Students and What Students Can Learn from Teachers

Edward P. J. Corbett

We do not always recognize that teaching is a two-way street. Like another familiar analogy—that of the pitcher and the catcher in baseball—the teaching process is often viewed as one in which one of the parties involved in the transaction is doing all of the transmitting and the other party is doing all the receiving. The common concept of the writer-reader relationship is similar: the writer does all the work; the reader just sits back and absorbs—or falls asleep.

Because I am a slow learner, it took me a long time to realize that teaching is a reciprocal process. A lot of sweating goes on on both sides of the podium. Moreover, a lot of learning ensues on both sides of the podium. For a long time, I thought I was the only one in the classroom who was expressing moisture through the pores and the only one in the classroom who was dispensing knowledge. Because I was a slow learner, it took me most of my professional career to realize that all along my students had been teaching me steadily and profusely. It is too late for me to radically alter my own attitudes and methods in the light of the epiphany I have experienced, but I can

A shorter version of this paper was first delivered at the Young Rhetoricians' Conference in Monterey, California, 22–24 June 1989.

make some reparation for my persistent myopia by passing on to younger teachers the instant insights I have gained from my revelation.

I might start out by talking first about the dividends that students can reap from contact with the teacher. After all, since most of us think of the teacher-student relationship as a one-way conduit, we might start with the obvious: the teacher has something to give the student.

The simplest and most general answer to the question "what can students learn from the teacher?" is that students can learn whatever the teacher knows that they do not know. Students may regard what the teacher knows as not worth the time or the effort required of them to gain that knowledge. But we all know that the judgments of young people about what is worth acquiring are sometimes erroneous. Even we senior citizens frequently misjudge the worth of the fruits that the world dangles before our eyes, so we cannot fault inexperienced youth for their misappraisals. But what we can say is that if students are not receptive to what the teacher has to offer simply because they have misjudged the value of the plum, they are the losers.

Until they learn otherwise, however, students should always presume that the teacher knows something that they do not know. After all, there are circumstances that warrant the presumption: usually the teacher has met certain certification standards; most of the time, the teacher is older and more experienced than the students. Part of the Oriental students' great reverence for the Teacher is due not only to the official certification of the teacher's wisdom but also to the respect that their culture has for older people.

From my vantage point now as an elderly person, I can honestly say that I never had a teacher who made my classroom experience a complete waste of my time and attention. I was frequently bored by a teacher. I was often baffled by a teacher. I was sometimes disenchanted by a teacher. And although today I still know who my memorable teachers were and still can tell you which ones I learned the most from, I still cannot say that I ever came away empty-handed from any teacher I ever had. On the contrary, I could tick off for you many experiences in my life where I felt I had been cheated of the expected dividends—experiences such as reading a book or seeing a play or going on a trip or viewing a television program.

I acknowledge that the teacher is not the font of all knowledge. The teacher is mainly a conveyor of knowledge and skills and just one of many repositories of knowledge. The big buzzing world around us may be the premier font of knowledge. But we desperately need a guide through the maze of that big buzzing world. There are many guides available to us—parents, clergy, close friends. But maybe the most reliable of the guides for hire is the teacher. We can thank whatever gods that be that in our culture a certain number of years of education are mandatory for all young people and that there are paid, certified teachers to conduct that education. And if those teachers know even a little bit more than we know, our relationship with them is bound to be profitable.

The point I have been trying to make is that we stand to learn something from any relationship where the other party knows something that we do not know. What we learn may be more or less valuable to us. And admittedly there will be times when what we learn from the other party will be deleterious to us. The person, for instance, who knows about and introduces us to the euphoric sensations of a chemical drug may ultimately prove to be a baneful influence on us. But at least we expect teachers to have only good goods to dispense to their charges. There can be some guarantee that the goods dispensed by the teacher will be good if the teacher has the kind of ethos we traditionally associate with the pedagogue.

It is that pedagogical ethos which leads me to a discussion of the second general benefit that students can derive from their contact with a teacher. The second benefit is the set of values—intellectual or cultural or moral values—that a teacher can convey to the students. I do not mean to suggest that teachers should be deliberate proselytizers. Teachers should exemplify values, not harangue their students about them. Teachers, like other professionals, go through a crucible in order to practice their profession. They want to win the privilege of standing in front of a room full of eager or apathetic students and engaging those students in some sort of intellectual exploration.

Teaching is the most private of the professions. Other professionals—doctors, lawyers, engineers—are exposed ultimately to public scrutiny and assessment. But once the teacher closes the door of the classroom, only God and the students—and maybe the teacher—know what goes on behind the closed door. That situation places a tremendous responsibility on teachers. Their integrity—and maybe the ultimate welfare of the students—is on the line. Mind you, they should not take advantage of that closed arena and indoctrinate their students verbally about any particular brand of religion or politics or way of life. However, they can hardly help transmitting some set of values just by their demeanor, their dress, their carriage, their speech patterns, their mere presence on the podium. For that reason, they must be what Quintilian said the ideal orator must be: a good man (or woman) skilled in speaking.

To my mind, being a genuinely good person is the greatest challenge for the teacher. All of us, merely because we are human, are fallible and peccable—and we frequently fall from grace. Nevertheless, when the genuinely good person falls from grace, there is somehow always a residue of nobility and inspiration. I am not suggesting that teachers have to be untarnished saints. Some of the great ones I have known have occasionally cussed like a sailor's parrot when their sensibilities were outraged. But I am asserting that teachers must be unswervingly conscientious, honest, and fair in their dealings with students.

That is the challenge: to be invariably conscientious, honest, and fair in dealing with students. Meeting that challenge may strike some of you as being an easy task, but for most of us, meeting that challenge is the hardest task of all. When I recollect my own practices as a teacher, I simply cringe at the thought of the many times in my career when I was not conscientious or honest or fair in dealing with my students. But I have known a few teachers who hewed unswervingly to that standard.

You have all read or heard somebody's testimony about a person who had profoundly affected his or her life. I have been amazed to discover how often the influential person mentioned in those testimonies has been a former teacher. I have more often heard that it was a teacher rather than a parent or a minister or a boss that turned somebody's life around.

I want all of you now to ask yourselves who had a great influence on the course of your life. Who pushed you in the direction that you eventually took? Who made you what you are today—for better or for worse? I wonder how many of you would answer, as I would, "A teacher."

In my case, it was a teacher of Greek whom I had in high school for at least one class all four years. I want to talk a bit about him because he exemplifies the kind of beneficent ethos I am talking about. He was a Ph.D. who preferred to teach in high school rather than in the university. He was filled with his subject, classical Greek, and he loved it as no other teacher I have ever been exposed to has loved the subject he or she was teaching. An elderly man in his early sixties, he walked two and a half miles to school every morning, and on the way he would recite to himself the hundreds of lines from Homer's *Iliad* or from Xenophon's *Anabasis* that he had committed to memory. If you think that we callow youth were not edified by this display of commitment to learning, you are sadly mistaken. In the breaks between classes, we would frequently exclaim to one another about the wonders of this man's stunning erudition.

This extraordinarily learned man gave us ridiculously high grades on our report cards, not because he was indifferent to intellectual standards but because he had learned along the way that high grades were a powerful incentive for young men to study their Greek. And he was right. We studied harder in that class than we did in the classes where we barely squeaked by with a B-minus. Maybe we *earned* those high grades because we studied hard.

And he was a good man, an exemplary man. I pronounce that judgment about him not because he was a priest but because he fairly exuded, unpretentiously but genuinely, moral and intellectual integrity. What an inspiration he was to us all! He did not preach to us, but by the example of his ethos he made us aspire to be solidly learned, and he made us ashamed of ourselves if we mortally or venially fell from grace in our personal lives. How can one measure what effect such a teacher had on the lives and the fortunes of his students? All I can say is that the effect was as profound as it was unmistakable.

Those are the principal things that students can learn from a teacher: a thirst and a respect for knowledge and a sterling set of intellectual and moral values. I wish I could give you the formula for how a teacher succeeds in promoting those objectives, but the formulation of such a procedure is the subject for another paper, a paper that I am not qualified to present. Instead, let us now consider the other side of the teacher-student relationship: what teachers can learn from students.

I can give a formula that will prepare teachers to learn whatever is to be learned from their students. The formula is easy to articulate but difficult to effectuate, but here it is: attune yourselves to the mind-set of your students. Anyone who has taught for even a few years has had the unsettling experience of alluding in the classroom to some putatively familiar event or personage and meeting with a scrim of glassy-eyed responses from the students. And the older you get as a teacher, the more often you meet with those blank responses. I remember how shocked I was the first time I got that kind of blank response from my students when I alluded to an event that was etched indelibly in my memory: Jack Ruby shooting Lee Harvey Oswald on live television. Now if you were to mention that 1963 world-class event in your classroom, you would not only have to describe the event but have to identify the two men involved in it.

I mention this common experience that teachers have of unresponsive responses from their students because it is the classic example of teachers broadcasting on a frequency quite different from the one their students are tuned to. The frequency metaphor is an apt one here because the baby boomers—and now their children—are, as Marshall McLuhan once reminded us, more "ear-oriented" than "eye-oriented." The private libraries of many of the college students of my generation were stocked with books; the private libraries of most students today are stocked with record albums or compact discs. The difference in what the different generations of college students treasure makes a profound difference in what students readily respond to. I won't go into the different cognitive dispositions brought on by one's repeated exposure to what McLuhan called the "hot media" and the "cool media," but I will mention that if teachers today just want to gain the attention of students in the classroom so that the students can be infused with the instruction prescribed by the syllabus, they are more likely to succeed if they resort to the medium of sound than to the medium of print. Even a message printed in billboard size is not going to distract teenagers from the enchantment of the Walkman cooing in their ears. I do not mean to suggest that older teachers have to abandon what edifies or enchants them and adopt what educates and entertains their young charges, but they do have to make an effort to discover and understand what turns their students on.

It is as natural for a gulf to develop between teachers and students as it is for a gulf to develop between parents and children. But if we do not strive to narrow that gulf, we will diminish our effectiveness as teachers and will foreclose any chance we might otherwise have of learning what our students have to teach us.

Again, I was a slow learner on this score, and I shouldn't have been, because by the time I was ten years into my teaching career, I had had considerable acting experience. It is a commonplace that one of the skills actors have to develop is the ability to put themselves into the shoes of the character they are playing and to act and think the way that character would. I did have some success in making that transformation of personalities on the stage, but it was a number of years before I realized that I had to make a similar kind of transformation in the classroom: I had to make an effort to put myself into the shoes—or, if you don't like that metaphor, into the disposition—of my students and to imagine how they were responding to what I was preaching or teaching. For a number of years, I kept exclaiming to my students about the mellifluous voice of Bing Crosby emanating from my old 78 rpm records, while they were responding to the rockabilly rhythms and gyrations of Elvis Presley on television. Just the fact that my students and I danced to a different rhythm created a gulf between us.

How do we get on our students' frequency? The surest way I know of is to have frequent conferences with the students. Many teachers, I am sure, have adopted the policy of inviting their students to their office for a conference about anything connected with the class. Some teachers have better luck with that policy than I have had. I have an office across the corridor from a colleague who gets a steady stream of students in response to that kind of standing policy. I must strike my students as an ogre; they do not come to confer with me in my office unless they are absolutely desperate for help.

There are some writing programs in this country that require instructors to hold a specified number of conferences with their students during the term. Don Murray's program at the University of New Hampshire mandated conferences with students on every writing assignment. A teacher in that program told me that when he first began teaching at the University of New Hampshire, he was skeptical about the efficacy of mandated conferences, but now he says that he cannot conceive of teaching a writing course in any other way. I discovered the efficacy of mandated conferences when I began teaching our technical writing course about ten years ago. The curriculum demanded that we require our students to confer with us at least twice in connection with the major report they have to write. I find these conferences so exhausting that I do not set up more than four of them on any one day of the school week.

But I have found these conferences so rewarding for me that I encourage my students to visit me more than twice during the term, and I would definitely establish a system of mandated conferences for any writing course I taught if such a system were not set by the director of the course. What makes these conferences rewarding for me is that they enable me to get a fix on my students: I learn a great deal about their backgrounds, about their strengths and weaknesses in several areas, about their problems, not only in connection with the assignment but in connection with their other classes and commitments, about their aspirations, about their personal lives—although I do not press any of my students for information about their personal lives if they do not want to talk about such matters. One would suppose that the succession of relatively brief conferences with students would soon blur in one's memory, but I have been surprised by how much I remember about each student right up to the end of the term. And best of all, I get so attuned to the mind-set of my students that I no longer exclaim in the classroom about the wonders of Bing Crosby's crooning when they are at that stage of their life where they are turned on by the singing of Madonna.

Another way to get attuned to your students' psyche is to put yourself in a situation where you are once again a beginning learner. Once we ourselves get away from being a student in the classroom, it is very easy for us to forget how baffling and frustrating a teacher's lecture or assignment can be for the neophyte. I had an awakening a number of years ago when I decided that I was going to learn how to play the banjo. Instead of going to a music teacher, I decided that I was going to get a book on how to play the banjo and hole up in my room to learn the intricacies of this glorious stringed instrument. I discovered that I had to start at square zero. I had everything to learn and only an instruction book to teach me. I went through a lot of trials and made a lot of errors, and my progress in acquiring the skill was slow and uncertain. I still haven't learned to play the banjo well enough to play for my friends.

But the chief fruit of that humbling experience is that I came to realize how students feel when they venture into a new area of learning, whether it be a class in literature or composition or chemistry or economics. And when I realized the bewilderment and frustration of the beginning learner, I was better able to adjust the level of my teaching to the temper of my audience.

Mimi Schwartz, who teaches at Stockton State College in New Jersey, reported in the Staffroom Interchange section of the May 1989 issue of *College Composition and Communication* about her experience in taking two creative writing courses for credit at Princeton University, one in fiction writing, the other in poetry writing. Like me, she had some salutary epiphanies as a result of becoming a student again. She said about her experience:

> I was surprised at my own vulnerabilities as a writer. Many of my fears, confusions, and needs were not so different from my younger counterparts' as I would have

predicted. Remembering "what it was like" as a student writer—and recording in my journal what worked and didn't work for me and for my classmates—has altered my teaching as well as my writing. (203–4)

Already a good teacher of writing, Mimi Schwartz has become a better teacher as a result of her experience, a teacher more sensitive to the needs, the insecurities, the bewilderments of her students. But we don't have to enroll in a formal class in order to renew the experience of a student having to write a paper. We can do what has been frequently recommended in journal articles and in convention talks: we can sit down and write the papers we assign to our students.

Another form of re-experiencing the role of the student is described by Patrick Dias in an article in *English Education*. Dias reported on an experiment in which he teamed up groups of two or three university pre-service teachers with groups of two or three secondary school students and required the pre-service teachers to work collaboratively—as students, not as teachers—with the students on all assignments. The results of that experiment were amazing to Dias, to his pre-service teachers, and to the high school students. Dias concluded that "a view of the act of teaching from the perspective of what teachers do needs to be complemented by an understanding and an experience of how that teaching is received by students. . . . It is the students who teach us about teaching" (208). One of the fruits, Dias claims, of the collaborative experience that he set up is that it forced the pre-service teachers "to recall and re-evaluate their past experiences as students" (207).

At one time, we all were needful, insecure, bewildered students. Furthermore, as students, most of us were far from being hotshots. We handed in some of our papers late; we sometimes gave our homework only a lick and a promise; we were often too proud to ask our teacher to clarify an assignment when we were baffled by it. Since it is easy for us to forget that when we were enrolled in elementary or secondary or college classes, we were no great shakes as students, we would do well to occasionally renew our sympathy and our empathy with our students by really or vicariously projecting ourselves back into the status of students. And then we will have disposed ourselves to learn what the students can teach us.

Our students can give us a new perspective on what we already know and can present us with enticing vistas of other worlds. They can remind us that studying is hard work, that all work and no play is stultifying, that stultification rots the mind. They can make us aware that mercy is frequently a restorative virtue, that intransigence is sometimes nothing more than unconscionable rigidity, and that a mere pat on the back can often be the impetus that impels one toward the finish line. But if we have kept our sensibilities sharp, we already *know* those truisms; we just have to be reminded of them—and our students are great reminders, if we will just pay attention to them. And if we pay attention to them they can also open up new vistas for us. It is easy for all of us to get locked up in our little circumscribed worlds. One of the ways to break out of those circumscribed worlds is to travel. Another way is to read about other worlds. Still another way for teachers to break out of their circumscribed worlds is to force themselves to become acquainted with the many diverse worlds that their students inhabit. As Terry Dean said in a recent article in *College Composition and Communication,* "Multicultural Classrooms, Monocultural Teachers," "With increasing cultural diversity in classrooms, teachers need to structure learning experiences that both help students write their way into the university and help teachers learn their way into student cultures" (23). Shirley Brice Heath was speaking of much the same thing when she said in her book *Ways with Words,*

> Unless the boundaries between classrooms and communities can be broken and the flow of cultural patterns between them encouraged, the schools will continue to legitimate and reproduce communities of townspeople who control and limit the potential progress of other communities who themselves remain untouched by other values and ways of life. (369)

In short, what students can teach their teachers is the paramount lesson that a rhetorician has to learn: that of all the elements which play a part in the communication process, audience is the most important. Teachers are defined by their students. What do I mean by that curious statement? Well, there are a number of ways in which it is true to say that students define their teachers. For instance, the successes of our students help to validate us as teachers. It is common for people to say of someone who has achieved some honor, "She was a student of so-and-so." That so-and-so teacher not only basks in the glory of that student but acquires a special kind of certification as a teacher.

But teachers are defined also by their ordinary students and by their remedial students. If we remain sensitive to the aspirations that our students entertain, to the stock of knowledge that they command, and to the cognitive skills that they possess, we will be disposed to make those adjustments in our teaching necessary to accommodate their expectations and their capacities. If we don't remain sensitive to the particular population of students that we have in the classroom in a particular semester, we will make unrealistic assignments, we will season our lectures with a sprinkling of jargon, and we will probably make a lot of wounding comments about our students' responses and performances.

What kinds of teachers are we? Our students can define us from the way we manifest ourselves in a particular class of a particular year. It is too bad that we can't eavesdrop on our students when they define us for other students outside the classroom. Hearing some of those definitions might help us to amend our ways. If we don't reach them, if we don't inspirit them, if we don't edify them, all our erudition, all our degrees, all our honors go for naught. We have to observe them, to listen to them, to intuit them. Remember what Patrick Dias said: "It is the students who teach us about teaching." If we keep our antennae tuned to their frequency, we can learn much from them that could convert us from being merely competent teachers to being great teachers. That's what mellowing is: the process whereby ordinariness matures into brilliance. Ripeness is all.

Recently I saw the movie *Dead Poets Society*, in which Robin Williams plays the part of a teacher of English in a New England prep school who uses some very unorthodox methods of teaching. In one scene, he jumps up on his desk in the classroom and asks the students, "Why am I standing up here?" When one of the students answers, "Because you want to be taller," Williams responds that he is standing on his desk not because he wants to be taller but because he wants to get a new perspective on the classroom and on his students. Then he jumps down from the desk and invites all of his students to jump up on the desk in turn and from that perch take a fresh look at the classroom and at their fellow students. Maybe the secret of maximizing the lessons that teachers can learn from students and the lessons that students can learn from teachers is for both parties to change perspectives on each other occasionally so that they can put themselves in a receptive disposition for learning and can become, to use the wonderful tautology, mutual friends.

Part II
Intuition and Institution

7

Critical Reflection, Change, and the Practice of a Theory of Composition

Christine R. Farris

It is the 10:30–11:30 hour in English 101. In one classroom, an instructor teaches the syllogism and then passes out a list of the approved topics for the argument paper. In another class, the instructor spends the first part of the hour on active and passive voice and then leads a discussion on the theme of suicide in an assigned short story by O. Henry. In another room, an instructor is "workshopping" a draft with the whole class, suggesting, along with his students, that the writer move beyond what the class has come to call "the list paper." Yet another instructor begins the period by asking students to read the "found poems" they have discovered over the weekend. He ends the period by explaining the grading system he has devised based on how earned run averages are calculated in baseball.

Are these instructors working across the decades from one another? Across the country? No, they work across the hall from one another in the same freshman composition program. Are the inconsistencies here cause for alarm? Before I conducted an ethnographic study of new composition instructors' theory and practice, I would have unequivocally said yes. A writing program may claim theoretical and practical consistency and nevertheless expose its graduate instructors to composition strategies grounded in what could be considered competing theories. While the program may appear to have in place a unified theory of composition, on closer examination, there is actually much difference. It is a difference, however, that I now believe can be the impetus for instructors' reflection on what they are doing when they teach composition. It is a difference that, if acknowledged, can be the basis for graduate instructor training that successfully integrates theory with practice—if we are willing to help new teachers of writing not just to change their classroom practice, but to reflect upon and reconstruct the theory that informed that practice.

While composition specialists and some seasoned instructors who keep up with the professional literature may adapt their practice to the theoretical turns that inform the so-called "paradigm shift" from product to process, for a long time we have had little information on the extent to which and in what ways the teaching of composition by new instructors is actually driven by theory. Many composition commentators who document and categorize theoretical changes in the profession have a tendency to lump practitioners, new and old alike, with theorists and researchers, assuming that all three are equally involved in a quest for the unified, the truest, or the most politically correct grand theory of composition.[1]

One of these commentators, James Berlin, has suggested that writing teachers too often make unconscious, eclectic pedagogical choices that are inescapably ideological. According to Berlin, a particular approach to composition is not just an emphasis; it is, and should be, a unified construct. In his frequently cited article "Contemporary Composition: The Major Pedagogical Theories," Berlin classifies pedagogical approaches according to their governing epistemology. "The way that writer, reality, audience and language are defined and related," he says, "will form a distinct world construct with distinct rules for discovering and communicating knowledge" and make for "specific directives about invention, arrangement, and style." He characterizes and traces the roots of his four pedagogical theories—Aristotelian, Current-traditional, Expressionist, and New Rhetorical—in order to argue that the approach of the New Rhetoricians "is the most intelligent and most practical alternative available, serving in every way the needs of our students." He is also "concerned," he says, that "writing teachers become more aware of the full significance of their pedagogical strategies" so as not to offer "contradictory advice about composing—guidance grounded in assumptions that simply do not square with each other" (766).

While I agree with Berlin that there is certainly a lot of unreflective eclecticism in composition teaching nowadays, I must question the extent to which this brand of typological analysis of seemingly unified theories can be applied to individual practitioners, especially to those who "practice" the most in this country—new graduate teaching assistants. Individual teachers' constructed theories are, of course, unique and complex. They are not ideal types that match the overly broad categories into which we might be tempted to place them. Even if writing teachers identify themselves as "Expressionists" or "New Rhetoricians," their day-to-day practice reveals contradictions, some, but not all, of which they are in the process of resolving.

After a year-long ethnographic study of how new composition teachers construct and change a theory and my subsequent experience teaching new graduate students in a composition pedagogy seminar, I am convinced that when we inquire into how composition theory informs practice, we need to look more closely at the beliefs of these *individual* writing teachers and at the *local* forces that shape them, not just at the larger theoretical and historical forces under revision in the discipline. This reflection on difference and consideration of contextual forces must be the basis of our training of new composition teaching assistants.

I agree with Berlin that composition teachers run the risk of offering contradictory advice about writing when they blithely introduce students to sentence combining, generative rhetoric of the paragraph, goal setting, dialectical notebooks, and collaborative group work all in the same course. But when we really look at the field of composition through the eyes and through the changing praxis of those who actually teach the most composition, the idea of a unified or an epistemologically or ideologically consistent theory is seriously called into question. We *can* ask, as Berlin and others have done: "Where is truth located in this rhetorical theory? What are the roles of writer, subject, audience, and language?" But the relationship between theory and practice involves more than just a distinction between where knowledge is located in several competing rhetorical worldviews. Instead, this relationship involves personal histories and local conditions, as well as global and historical circumstances. And these local conditions include institutional requirements, student resistance, and maybe even the disillusionment some new teachers experience with the whole composition teaching enterprise.

When, as researchers, administrators, mentors, and professors of composition studies, we examine the beliefs and practices of new teachers in the full context of their past and present histories and the programs for which they work, it is not unified "versions of reality" that we are likely to find, but theories in flux. Writing teachers must work out of the theory they already have while at the same time they reflect upon that theory's usefulness in shaping practices that will solve the daily problems they encounter in teaching students to write. Practice, reflection, and change produce a continuous dialectical process of encountering and attempting to resolve contradictions. The relationship between theory and practice may thus be described as one that strives for unity but never achieves it.[2]

Of course, few new composition teachers are composition theorists per se. Most of them are part-time instructors or graduate teaching assistants who are relatively new to teaching and who do not attend the annual Conference on College Composition and Communication or read *College English* or *Research in the Teaching of English*. They will not necessarily go on to specialize in composition and rhetoric, even though, at most large state universities, except for an occasional faculty member, they do *all* the teaching of composition. While I deliberately introduce new teaching assistants to a substantial amount of theory (James Berlin's articles among them) in my graduate seminar, I do not assume they are *tabulae rasae* when it comes to the teaching of writing. They do not come to our programs lacking theories of discourse. In my interactions with these graduate initiates in my *own* discipline I must remind myself of the Paolo Freire dictum that I have no trouble recalling when I work with faculty teaching writing in *other* disciplines: begin where they are.

I have not found that new graduate teachers ever sit passively through an orientation session or a graduate seminar, assimilate information about the teaching of writing, and then choose or construct a full-blown theory from which to teach. Instead, their implicit theories constructed from their experiences as students, tutors, journalists, poets, and parents constitute a worldview that influences but does not necessarily stabilize or categorize—developmentally, epistemologically, or ideologically—how they will teach writing. They pull, therefore, from the composition tradition somewhat erratically and reflect each in his or her own way the competing theories operating simultaneously in the field. Through the dynamic activity of teaching and self-reflection, they continue to question, to resolve difference, and to work toward what they perceive as meaningful change.

My research study of new graduate teaching assistants came about because, in wanting to know more about how theory informs practice, I decided to look at those people who are thrown into the practice and how they are able or not able to make choices and act in relation to what are often considered competing theories. If you want to understand what a science is, says Clifford Geertz, look not just at the theories or the findings, and certainly not at what its apologists say about it; look at what the practitioners of it do. And so I did.[3]

I chose an ethnographic methodology for my year-long study because it enabled me to examine the pedagogies of new composition teachers not as examples of discrete competing theories, not as developmental (moving from teacher-centered to student-centered concerns), not as effective or ineffective, but as personal, contextual, dynamic, changing phenomena. I wanted to know out of what personal beliefs and from what traditional or new ideas they operated in constructing their courses. If and when their teaching changed from one term to the next, what was the relation of theory to practice? I also wanted to know how the required textbook, Donald Murray's *Write to Learn,* did or did not function as a theory of composition for the new teachers, who had to situate themselves and their teaching in relation to it.

I collected data on six teaching assistants for three consecutive academic quarters, eventually narrowing the final analysis to four. The three methods I used to collect data about theory construction and changes in teaching practice included collection of classroom materials, classroom observation, and elicitation of instructors' thoughts about the teaching of writing.[4] Class materials I collected included syllabi, assignments, handouts, and some whole sets of graded student papers, as well as student course evaluations. I spent two to three sessions per quarter observing each TA's classroom, where I took field notes and attempted to understand the theory or theories of writing operating within it.

I must point out that I was not in an administrative or supervisory position when I conducted this research. Administrative or faculty status does not afford one a disinterested perspective from which to view a writing program. Even if an administrator's purpose were to understand ethnographically the praxis of an instructor in her charge, the potential for the observation to become evaluative would interfere. However, in my more recent position closer to composition program "management," I continue to use some of my research techniques as the basis for TAs' critical pedagogy. Because I learned so much from my "thick description" of each teacher's classroom

community, I now see ethnographic observation as a means for
reflection on practice, a technique I recommend as a training tool
for both supervisors and peers. More important, however, than my
visiting TAs' classes twice a semester can be their visiting one another's classes, taking field notes, and sharing with one another (nonjudgmentally) their observations over time. I am not talking about observations of how their peers make use of the blackboard but about
observations of how fellow instructors' approaches to composition
play out in their classrooms. Time and again, TAs have told me that
they did not understand what it was *they* believed about the teaching
of writing—what *their* "theory" was—until they attempted to analyze
what someone else apparently believed about "good writing" or what
someone else was trying to get across to students in order to solve a
writing problem. Their experiences have certainly echoed mine as the
ethnographer who simultaneously constructs and comes to know
what she believes in the very process of constructing and understanding "the other."

In order to capture the ongoing reflection in which TAs in my
study were engaged from day to day, I asked them to fill out daily
class log sheets adapted from a form used by Ronald Lunsford
("Teaching"). They recorded answers to questions that asked what
concepts they were attempting to get across that day; what, if any,
reading and writing were done for the class; how class time was
spent; what they felt best about; and what, if anything, troubled
them about the class meeting; and, also, what comments from students stood out in their memory. In the second quarter of the study,
wanting to focus on critical moments that could result in changes in
theory and practice, I added an additional question that asked what,
if anything, they would do differently next time. This question proved
to be a key resource for my understanding of how unmet expectations
in practice often led to adjustments in what TAs believed about the
teaching of writing.

In my graduate seminars for new TAs I have continued to use these
class logs as springboards for class discussion and as data for what I
call the "reflective inquiry" paper. I ask the students to focus on "a
problem" they see in the teaching of writing and then go through
what might be the beginning stages of composition research—reflection on what has occurred, worked, not worked, and changed in their
own practice and, consequently, in their theory of composition.

During twelve hours of interviews with each TA in the research
study, I asked clarification questions that referred back to the class

logs they were keeping for me and to my classroom observations. The TAs talked about the particulars of their essay assignments, students, teaching strategies, the required Donald Murray textbook, and their changing beliefs. My emphasis in later interviews was on what they felt was changing in both their theory of composition and in their teaching practice. Now, as someone who listens to a lot of new TA failures, successes, and soul-searching, I find this focused interview to be a valuable way to work on change. On any given day, I find myself guiding TAs back and forth from practice to theory to practice again. Often new TAs with whom I work will want to abandon altogether a particular strategy they are using, such as peer response groups, and I will get them to reflect on the particulars and not rush to a generalization about the usefulness of collaborative activities. I want TAs to be confident that no matter what they try in the classroom, they *have* a theory they are testing, adjusting, and working out of all the time.

I will concentrate here on the theory construction of three of the TAs from whom I learned much over the course of my year's study. Martha was a poet and professional feature writer who returned to graduate school. Robert was the only participant who intended to specialize in composition and rhetoric. Heather was a fiction writer in the creative writing program. The year I followed them was a particularly interesting one in which to examine the relationship between theory and practice in that the program was in transition and temporarily without a permanent rhetoric/composition-trained director. (A faculty member whose specialty was literature took over for the year while a search was conducted for a permanent director.) TAs did have access to a weekly syllabus compiled from syllabi distributed in years past and updated by a senior TA to accompany the textbook by Donald Murray, which was new to the program. The syllabus included syntheses of several approaches to the composing process, numerous suggestions for teaching invention, arrangement, and style, and advice about grading and miscellaneous procedures. Suggested topics for formal essays were included in the syllabus and adopted by the TAs in my study. That year, apart from the guidance provided by the syllabus and two senior TAs, new TAs were, for the most part, on their own.

What I found common to the TAs in my study was a process of simultaneously adjusting their theory and practice, a sort of continuous process of tacking back and forth between their experiences teaching writing and their interpretation of those experiences in order to resolve differences, particularly differences that arose when their beliefs and expectations about writing confronted events in the classroom, students' performance on papers, the textbook, the program guidelines, and theoretical ideas raised in their graduate coursework.

It is my sense that the self-reflection thrust upon them by my year-long study assisted the TAs in making their implicit theories more explicit and flexible. Frequently it was in the very act of telling me what had or had not worked successfully or of filling out the class logs that they clarified their theories by articulating what wasn't working and what they would do differently in practice next time. In modifying specific teaching strategies, they also adjusted what they now believed should be the goals of a composition teacher and an expository writing program. In using their theories, both to teach and to reflect critically, they not only retained what they found to be successful strategies, but also sought explanations and alternatives for what they felt to be their failures.

For instance, Martha, by the end of the school year, had come to realize that most students would not love writing as she, a poet and journalist, did. With that realization came the adjustment of her rationale for class assignments and activities. She changed her thrust from an "anyone can write and love it" approach, one she originally felt that the Murray text endorsed, to an emphasis that she later believed represented a closer reading of Murray—that writers, as craftspeople, choose from a variety of useful strategies and tools which they can try, use again, or discard. Chief among these, she felt, was getting across to students that "writing is rewriting."

While she no longer felt that she needed to function as an advocate of writing as a vocation, Martha's beliefs about the value of expressive writing, particularly as a means of self discovery, resulted for a long time in a continued emphasis on the narration of personal experience more than on the critical interpretation of experience. In gradually adjusting her expectations for students as writers, Martha simultaneously adjusted her understanding of the textbook, her assignments, and her goals for the course, which by the end of the term were somewhat more technical than artistic: "to give students a taste of different strategies, focuses, writing styles, including at least one assignment on which everyone will do well." The change in her view of the writer as someone who seeks pleasure in self-discovery and expression into someone who discovers her own writing process, style, and voice to complete a task was gradual, subtle, but nevertheless, as Berlin would have it, more than a shift in practical classroom emphasis; it was a change in her personal theory of composition.

Robert also discovered limitations in his working theory of composition, finding fault in what he originally called his "psychological" model of the composing process, which emphasized the sovereignty of the writer, when he didn't see any change in the quality of his students' writing. Early in the school year, feeling theoretically aligned with Donald Murray, Robert used many of the textbook's strategies for examining students' writing processes and the choices they make when they brainstorm, draft, and revise. Robert wanted to give students what he felt would be "authority over their own writing." Nevertheless, Robert found their essays "lackluster, underdeveloped, and pointless."

This finding led Robert to refine his theory at the same time that he adjusted his practice. He designed what he called the "essay graph," a structural diagram of students' papers, to demonstrate the need he saw for them to devote time to a fuller and more coherent development of ideas. Later, feeling even more need for work on fulfilling reader expectations and less for work on the needs of the individual writer, Robert expanded the use of peer critiques into what he called "class forums," one- and two-hour critique sessions on drafts. Rather than rejecting a theory of composition and adopting a new one outright, it could be said that, like Martha, he too tested the extent to which his personal theory was workable in the new environment and then modified his theory to fit the practice he felt *was* working. Robert did not abandon his original psychological "writer-based" approach to invention, but by the end of the year, group critique on both drafts and final papers had become his central pedagogical activity, as he moved steadily from an emphasis on a writer's own process to an emphasis on the effects finished products have on readers and, consequently, to a more sociocontextual theory of composition.

It becomes apparent when one observes the relationship between theory and practice in individual teachers that part of their critical reflection involves not only a testing and a broadening of a theory out of which to teach composition, but also an inevitable and necessary *limiting* function. New instructors, in order to survive, must narrow and focus what they will teach about writing. To the extent that the structure we erect rules us, we could say that a personal theory of composition is deterministic. If Martha believes that one of her chief functions as a writing teacher is to elicit honest emotion and recall of sensory detail in students' writing, what students will write and learn and be evaluated on in her course is bound up by that emphasis on individual perception and personal discovery. For Martha, the poet/feature writer, it was always the *recording* of experience more than the critical *interpretation* of experience, to use Henry Giroux's distinction (*Theory and Resistance* 220), that continued, despite her modifications, to receive her highest priority.

It is inevitable that the changes the TAs made from week to week or from academic quarter to quarter were guided not only by the *limits* they had set for themselves and that the program had set for them, but also by the *limitations* of their personal theories, by what Kenneth Burke would call their "terministic screens."

For instance, Martha became frustrated that Donald Murray's book included no readings for students, so she began bringing in plays, poems, book reviews, and provocative quotes to stimulate discussion and the writing of opinion essays. But her remarks in class and her comments on students' papers indicated that even though her later assignments invited analysis and critique, she was evaluating these later papers according to the same criteria—that is, the literal perception of the concrete, objective world—that she had stressed in the early assignments that called for narration and description of personal experience.

Even though Robert's belief in the importance of peer interaction replaced his former belief in the authority of the writer, he continued to struggle with his authority as teacher in his own classroom. As his course goals broadened to include not only an awareness of the writing process but a view of writing as "a real act of communication in real situations," he found himself taking back some of the authority in the class that he had so wanted to surrender to the students when the course emphasis was on the writer or on responses from peers. As he made students more aware of discourse conventions and readers' expectations of form in different genres, he also found himself doing a lot of the talking in the "democratic" class forums. He felt it necessary to keep a rein on what theoretical standards informed the course, what group standards were evolving and being carried over from one assignment to the next, and what student progress was being made. Ultimately, Robert, not the group, determined the standards for "good" writing in the course.

Perhaps because of the limitations imposed on them by the contexts in which they work—program requirements, textbooks, syllabi with recommended or required assignments, assessment efforts, not to mention the writing abilities of students—instructors' attempts at critical reflection and the reconciliation of differences may not always make for satisfied teaching or lead to productive change.

Heather, the fiction writer in my study, indicated that her ability to use Donald Murray's self-discovery approach to the writing process, which would have students choosing and developing their own "open" topics, was hampered in her course by the constraints imposed by the program: the requirement of eight "closed" assignments with topics suggested in the program syllabus (e.g., "The Interview" or "A Subject on Which You Are an Authority"). As soon as the purpose, audience, and sources for assignments were no longer "open," according to Heather, classroom, peer response group, and writing conference discussion no longer centered on individual student writers' discovery, meaning-making, or revision processes. Instead, Heather felt, all dialogue with her students became product-centered, concerned with the conventions, formats, and expectations integral to each particular "closed" assignment. Like Robert, Heather found herself having to negotiate students' "what do you want?" into "what do readers expect?" in order to avoid a clash between textbook and syllabus.

Heather's more difficult struggle with reconciling her theory with the practice dictated by the program came late in the school year. Over three quarters, she had become increasingly frustrated with her students' failure to think critically—to "recognize the underlying assumptions and implicit values in what they were writing." By the end of the winter quarter, she was convinced that her students were deliberately writing to persuade her they were not committed to anything, that not only did they choose *not* to have an opinion on something like nuclear arms, but that they felt it was their *right* not to have an opinion. After some unsuccessful attempts to broaden student perspectives on various issues at the invention stage through the use of Burke's pentad, Heather eventually gave in to what she felt was the "contextless" nature of the freshman course. "It is impossible for us to have any real issues in common that anyone knows anything about," she said.

Heather eventually modified what she came to feel was Murray's excessively subjective approach ("writing what you already know") into her version ("you don't know as much as you think you know"). Instead of calling for students to consider "multiple perspectives" to which they had never been exposed, Heather's solution was to have students "set their own texts in motion" by considering multiple perspectives or contradictions in themselves. "The trouble is," she said, "I've adjusted my theory, but I haven't figured out how to get the students to do that. They still define and redefine concepts unproblematically—the way they *want* them to be, not the way they are, were, or might be."

While Heather was able to devise from her own teaching, from her experience as a writer, and from her theoretical exploration a personal theory more complex than the one presented to her by the Murray textbook, she had a more difficult problem than did Martha and Robert: relating her theory to a complex level of pedagogy within the contextual framework of the course and the department's composition program. At the end of her first year in the program, she decided that college teaching was not for her.

It would seem that hope for more effective writing programs and for teacher change lies in bringing instructors' theories to a level of self-criticism which will result in ongoing reflection that is theory-directed. But such action need not be defined as unified or a movement toward an ideal.

What I have learned from my research is that as TAs confront from week to week what it is they are trying to do, they need opportunities to reflect upon and synthesize their personal theories with those underlying the writing program for which they work, with those of their peers, and with those of professional composition theorists and textbook authors. In the program in which I have worked for the last three years, we have instituted weekly mentor group meetings in addition to the required seminar in composition theory and practice. In both the seminar and the meetings with the mentors (faculty members and senior TAs), new TAs thrash out what is working and not working, share good and bad assignments, observe one another nonjudgmentally, and, probably more than anything else, attack, modify, and expand upon the textbook and the program syllabus they are required to use. Midterm and final reviews of students' portfolios to establish writing proficiency are also conducted in mentor groups. Like other requirements in the freshman program, portfolio review is mandated from above, though we encourage as much as possible group "ownership" of the review process through holistic criteria for proficiency and ongoing discussion of the changes TAs want to make in their teaching as a result of reading hundreds of portfolios.

While the mentor group is a good place to introduce and reinforce the new directions that a writing program may wish to take, one important lesson I have learned is that, despite the pressures of assessment and accountability that we face, it is not humanly possible or even desirable, when employing perhaps fifty to one hundred graduate teaching assistants and part-timers, to expect total theoretical and pedagogical consistency. In fact, my findings seem to indicate that an internally consistent composition theory and practice may be the consequence of a particularly secure "terministic screen," such that limited goals for teaching writing may yield consistent but limited results.

I remember Bill Irmscher describing the difference among TAs' approaches to teaching composition as a "healthy eclecticism," and in that phrase I will always hear his tolerance for the individual processes that TAs inevitably go through to discover and trust their teaching selves. The danger of an unhealthy eclecticism that refuses to value one approach over another is that it can lead to indifference in teachers and in programs. Rather than just tolerating difference, we need to view it as the impetus for reflection, and thus as the key to change, but still as difference that cannot necessarily be integrated into a unified whole. Surely it is not out of one consistent ideology but only out of a continuing reflection on difference that we change. It is the rich complexity and not the dichotomy of difference that we need to keep in mind as we continually reshape composition programs and train new teachers.

Notes

1. I refer to Lester Faigley's categories of Expressivist, Cognitivist, and Social, as set forth in his article "Competing Theories of Process: A Critique and a Proposal"; James Berlin's categories of Objective, Subjective, and Transactional as outlined in *Rhetoric and Reality;* and C. H. Knoblauch's categories of Ontological, Objectivist, Expressionist, and Sociological, as described in "Rhetorical Constructions: Dialogue and Commitment."

2. This is a dialectical process of critical self-reflection described similarly by George Kelly in a *Theory of Personality: The Psychology of Personal Constructs;* by Kenneth Burke in his discussion of the individual's capacity to use language to "circle back upon himself" (*Rhetoric of Religion* and elsewhere); and by Robert P. Parker in his

work on the changing beliefs of new writing teachers ("Writing Courses for Teachers: from Practice to Theory").

3. This study is described in detail in my doctoral dissertation, "Constructing a Theory of Composition: An Ethnographic Study of Four New Teaching Assistants in English," University of Washington, 1987.

4. The combination produced a corroborative effect, or triangulation of data, that contributed to internal validity and allowed me to cite related evidence from several sources: myself as participant-observer; the TAs, both in interviews and in the classroom; the students; the course materials; and student papers.

8

P*racticing Theory/Theorizing Practice*

Anne Ruggles Gere

Consider *theory*. Adjectives used to describe it often include "systematic," "rational," and "professional." Within the field of composition studies, advanced undergraduate classes and graduate seminars enact theories regularly. Emphasis on connections with classical rhetoric lends the theoretical version of composition studies prestige as well as a systematic approach wrought from the traditional parts or types of rhetoric. Consideration of rhetoric's complicated relationship to logic provides a rational perspective, one that undergirds varying approaches to invention, style, discourse, or evaluation. Instructors in these theoretical courses are usually recruited from the ranks of senior professors in English departments. These instructors, motivated by the generativity characteristic of their professional status, use the course to recruit a certain number of students to pursue graduate work in composition studies.

Now consider *practice*. Adjectives applied to it often include "ad hoc," "unsystematic," and "amateurish." The freshman writing program typically enacts the practice of composition studies. Here instructors, faced with the exigencies of initiating freshmen into the academic community, seize upon strategies that "work," prizing classroom effectiveness over systematic approaches. Goaded by the demands of colleagues that the writing "problems" of freshmen be eliminated, these instructors develop file folders full of handouts that address problems of specific students, even though the students who come along next semester will have different problems. Directors of these writing programs, constrained by limited budgets and shifting enrollments, often hire a large number of part-time and/or temporary instructors. Whether recruited from graduate programs in English or other disciplines, these instructors typically share limited preparation in composition studies.

While admittedly reductive, these portrayals of theory and practice in composition studies capture an essential dilemma facing the field today. As composition studies has moved toward scholarly respectability within the past couple of decades, it has created an ever-expanding division between theory and practice. When positions for directors of writing programs began to emerge in the 1950s, most chairs of English departments assumed that willingness, rather than special training, qualified faculty to direct a writing program. Concern in these programs centered on practice, and directors and instructors alike concentrated on how to teach writing to increasing numbers of students. In subsequent years directors of writing programs, emboldened by increased numbers and by the emergence of professional publications and organizations, moved to establish academic respectability for their work. Such a move required that composition extend its concerns beyond practice and deal with theoretical questions. With this move toward theory came a need for a more systematic approach to the field. Accordingly, courses and eventually graduate programs in composition studies began to emerge. Students trained in these programs have a much more substantial background in the field, but they do not automatically have the concern for practice that characterized earlier generations of composition faculty.

While the development of professionalism, publication, and graduate training in composition studies is to be applauded, the resulting shape of the field raises questions about where we are headed. What is the relationship between the theory studied in advanced courses and the practices of instruction carried out in our writing programs? What are the implications of the developing professionalism of composition studies? Can a rapprochement between theory and practice be effected?

Before we look for closer connections between theory and practice, we might consider the implications of the division between the two. Is it really bad for composition studies to move in these two directions? Perhaps the best answer comes from history. As Donald Stewart has documented, during the late nineteenth century, when composition was first taking its place in higher education, the "Harvardization" of composition won out. The 1891 Harvard committee (composed of alumni from the business community), which was concerned with surface features of writing, gained dominance over rhetoricians such as Fred Newton Scott, who took a more complex and rhetorically based view of freshman writing. This privileging of amateur views created a stronghold for practice. The Harvardization of composition contributed to the distance between theory and practice in our field. Cut off from theory, composition languished into mechanistic operations which could be taught or administered by anyone, and were.

To be sure, composition studies today does not face the same kind of domination by nonacademics as it did when the Harvard Committee made its report, but the number of nonspecialists who currently teach in and administer writing programs does raise questions about composition's status in the academy. The dependence of universities upon teaching assistantships to support graduate students guarantees a large cadre of instructors who cannot be described as possessing theoretical sophistication, even if they have participated in a required workshop or seminar. At two- and four-year colleges, where most literature faculty teach composition routinely, there may be one or two individuals who claim expertise in composition, but the majority practice without significant theoretical background, and the same is true for part-time and temporary instructors of composition. The guidelines of the CCCC's *Statement of Principles and Standards for the Postsecondary Teaching of Writing* suggest ways to alleviate some of the difficulties created by practice-dominated composition. But the numbers of students requiring instruction dictate that it will never be possible for all writing classes to be taught by someone with graduate work in composition studies.

The fact that some composition practice will necessarily be enacted by individuals lacking theoretical sophistication can seem, in light of normative English department standards, a liability. How, for example, would colleagues specializing in the Renaissance react to assigning Shakespeare courses to individuals who had never undertaken graduate study of Shakespeare? As Gerald Graff demonstrates, the survival and growth of English studies in the academy depended upon specialization, a specialization tied to theory rather than practice. Advocates of what Graff terms the generalist position, a group that tended to privilege practice over theory, lost out to specialists. However, even as he documents the history of specialization in English, Graff points to its liabilities, particularly in regard to its connection with professionalism.

Because it developed later than the literature branch of English studies, composition can benefit from literature's errors, and one such benefit might be to consider the influence of professionalism upon the practice-theory relationship. As Burton Bledstein explains, the development of universities in this country coincided with and supported the growth of professionalism. The middle class of the late nineteenth century assumed that educated knowledge was the beginning of power and that power was the source of spiritual and material riches (30). This class developed a hierarchical view of culture, one that affirmed competition and assigned high value to verbal contests. Just as they developed specialized uses of space, such as the baseball stadium and the department store, so too people of the Victorian period developed the concept of specialized individuals or professionals. These professionals, identified by specialized knowledge, distinguished themselves from mere practitioners by their theoretical sophistication. Accordingly, the growth of professionalism fostered (and continues to foster) the division between practice and theory.

Professionalism divides practice and theory because it operates on principles of exclusion and separation. From its earliest stages, professionalism has served individuals' needs for social status and economic power. Thanks to the specialized training and credentialing provided by university education, professionals claim social privileges and economic rewards not accorded the rest of the population. The specialized training provided by the university draws its authority on theory, and merging theory with practice threatens to diminish or destroy the social and economic privilege or, as Magali Larson puts it, "the inequality of status and closure of access in the occupational order" (xvii) that marks professionalism. Accordingly, members of the composition studies community, anxious to affirm their professional status, have begun to emphasize theory at the expense of practice.

Teacher research offers a way to reverse this trend toward division between practice and theory in composition studies. To date, most discussions of teacher research have concentrated on elementary and secondary school classrooms, but the dominant theme of teacher empowerment in these discussions undercuts the exclusionary aspects of professionalism. Glenda Bissex and Richard Bullock claim that teacher research transforms classrooms into sites of inquiry and expertise: "No longer dispensers of curricula designed by 'experts' from universities, textbook companies, or their school districts, these teachers become experts themselves, bringing knowledge and confidence to their teaching and showing that they are professional educators to be respected within schools and without" (xi). Marion Mohr and Marion Maclean assert that the hyphenated term *teacher-researcher* "implies a contrast between traditional assumptions about educational research and assumptions about teachers. Outside the university, teachers are not usually researchers, and researchers are not usually teachers" (3). Nancy Martin, in a collection edited by Dixie Goswami and Peter Stillman, notes: "Traditionally research is university guided" (27). Shirley Brice Heath, for example, describes how she taught a university course in which teachers learned to "become ethnographers of their own and others' interactions and to put to use knowledge about the different ways of learning and using language" (265–66). In highlighting these distinctions between universities as producing or guiding research and schools as consuming or receiving it, these advocates of teacher research call attention to the (undesirable) distinction between the two: the school is the site of practice while the university provides the theory that guides that practice. Or, as James Britton puts it, "Teaching is something we *do;* research findings are something we come to *know*" (l8). Teacher research, then, acknowledges the practice-theory dichotomy in order to remove it.

One way to remove the practice-theory dichotomy is to embody both in a single individual, and this is one of the claims frequently made for teacher research. Bissex argues that a teacher-researcher is a "more complete teacher," one who integrates knowing and doing, and she concludes with the personal observation that "if teacher research had been on the horizon ten years ago, I might still be in a classroom myself rather than having been driven to choose between knowing and doing" ("What Is" 5). Heath describes the reflective quality teachers developed as they began to examine their own practices: "For many, seemingly simple insights into their past classroom behaviors and attitudes opened the way for curricular reforms and modified teaching practices" (270). Thus, the teachers integrated theory and practice. Ann Berthoff urges the importance of "the kind of theory that is generated in dialogue among teachers" (*Making of Meaning* 30) and asserts that the reflections and reformulations of practitioners will shape research and theory in productive ways. Mohr and Maclean claim that the teacher-researcher who integrates theory and practice becomes "a teacher who observes, questions, assists, analyzes, writes and repeats these actions in a recursive process that includes sharing their results with their students and with other teachers" (4). Worthy as this kind of integration is, it starts from the premise that two entities—in this case theory and practice—are essentially different. In this view the appropriate metaphor to describe the ideal practice-theory relationship is one of "bridge" or "connection." The teacher-researcher who incorporates practice and theory creates a bridge between the two.

One explanation for the dichotomous view of theory and practice lies in the level of analysis in discussions of teacher research. That is, these discussions concentrate on methodology and do not extend to issues of epistemology. Mohr and Maclean, for example, urge qualitative, descriptive, and hypothesis-generating methods: "Traditional educational research, based on the experimental, hypothesis-testing model with its limited variables, has not always served teachers well" (4). Bissex, noting that the statistical approach dominant in much educational research comes from the physical sciences, claims, "A research approach appropriate, for example, in physics may not be appropriate to the study of human beings" ("What Is" 10). She goes on to advocate case study methodology as a better alternative. Goswami and Stillman open their collection by asserting, "We don't question the value of quantitative research in education, but in this book we take seriously the notion that teachers and students are able to formulate questions about language and learning, design and carry out inquiries, reflect on what they have learned, and tell others about it" (preface). Heath, true to her background in anthropology, advocates ethnography as the best method for teacher-researchers.

While it is important to question dominant methodologies and to urge the acceptance of new ones more consonant with teachers' goals and experiences, mere tinkering with methodologies is not sufficient. Teacher research can benefit composition studies if it moves beyond issues of method and considers the underlying epistemology. Methods are merely manifestations of the epistemology or way of knowing that makes them possible. Accordingly, practice and theory in composition studies will remain divided as long as questions of method obscure issues of what and how we know.

In his *Actual Minds, Possible Worlds*, Jerome Bruner, drawing on Vygotsky's theory of language, asserts that the language of education is "the language of culture creating, not of knowledge consuming or knowledge acquisition alone" (133). Bruner's distinction between "culture creating" and "knowledge acquisition" suggests two different epistemologies. The one, based on positivism, conceives of knowledge as a preexisting entity to be consumed or taken in by the learner.

This is the scientific view of knowledge on which our universities were founded. During the latter part of the nineteenth century, when universities in this country were taking shape, the positivism and scientific knowledge prominent in German universities received emphasis here as increasing numbers of American graduate students received training in Germany. Positivist scientific knowledge thus became privileged in our universities.

Composition studies owes its emergence to the domination of science because science diminished the power of the classical curriculum and gave increased importance to facility in English. Charles Eliot, who shaped Harvard's elective system and English in secondary schools because of his work on the Committee of Ten, personified this perspective. He argued that education should foster the student's development of systematic reasoning power and capacity to classify, to categorize, to draw inferences, and thereby to be armed against "succumbing to the first possible delusions or sophism he or she may encounter" (426). Eliot's enumeration demonstrates how university education incorporated a positivist epistemology.

The other epistemology suggested by Bruner's distinction conceives of knowledge as something created, not preexisting. Generally categorized under the rubric of "social constructionist," this view of knowledge assumes that knowledge does not concern itself with accuracy of representation so much as it does with what Richard Rorty calls "social justification of belief" (170). Bruner's description of education as the *language* of culture creating underlines the centrality of language in this conception of knowledge. In the positivist view, language serves as the medium or vehicle through which knowledge is transmitted, but the social constructionist view places language at the center of knowledge because it constitutes the means by which ideas can be developed and explored. Recent discussions of composition, particularly those by Kenneth Bruffee and Karen Burke Lefevre, demonstrate how theories derived from this epistemology can shape practice. They show how it changes processes of invention and even processes of writing itself.

Because there is little self-consciousness about epistemology among teacher-researchers, we can assume that the dominant form is positivist because positivism remains dominant enough to be invisible. One clear indication of this appears in Mohr and Maclean's discussion of validity and reliability. Even though they, like other teacher-researchers, assert that their work emphasizes description and hypothesis generation rather than proving hypotheses, they embrace a scientific view of knowledge as they discuss issues of validity and reliability. First, Mohr and Maclean identify teacher-researchers with "all researchers," a move which establishes a relationship to the scientific tradition and its positivistic concept of knowledge (62). They go on to identify eight characteristics that lend validity to teacher-researcher work. Next they explain how an individual study can achieve validity and reliability for one context, and then they state: "Eventually, the issue of reliability may be addressed best by analyzing collections of teacher-researchers' studies" (64). They go on to claim that "a kind of reliability exists in studies that are context-specific, like those of teacher-researchers" (64) and that reports of these studies can provide "generalizable 'truths'" (64). This concern with truth and with reliability and validity in general demonstrates how a positivist view of knowledge can pervade teacher research, even when the goals and methods of this research lack consonance with positivism. To invoke the metaphor of this collection, positivism threatens to throw teacher research off balance because it undercuts its essential nature.

A social constructionist view of knowledge, one that conceives of education as the language of creating culture rather than isolating the truth, can, alternatively, create a context in which teacher research establishes a common ground for practice and theory. Donald Schon makes this point when he identifies the difference between positivism and *reflection-in-action*. Technical rationality, Schon's term for the positivist view of knowledge, works effectively when problems need to be solved, when the one best means to established ends needs to be identified. But when there is "contention over multiple ways of framing the practice role" (41)—as there is in composition studies—the positivist approach fails. The more effective approach, what Schon calls "reflection-in-action," does not assume that knowledge is an entity to be discovered, but that the practitioner—whether a teacher or a baseball player—constructs knowledge during the process of doing something.

The mode of reflection-in-action varies according to the situation and the background of the practitioner, but whatever the mode, it enables the practitioner to "cope with the troublesome 'divergent' situations of practice" (62). As Schon puts it, "When someone reflects-in-action, he becomes a researcher in the practice context. He is not dependent on the categories of established theory and technique, but constructs a new theory of the unique case" (68). This "theory of the unique case" does not concern itself with "truth" or with scientific issues of validity or reliability. Rather, it values the knowledge of the specific context. Undergirded with this epistemology, teacher research can transform the relationship between theory and practice.

This epistemology transforms the theory-practice relationship because it diminishes the kind of professionalism that accompanied the emergence of universities invested in the scientific tradition. The professionalism credentialed and legitimated by university-bred positivism provides a means of sorting individuals into hierarchical relationships based on distinctions between knowing and doing or theory and practice. Despite its hegemony of theory, such professionalism is not invulnerable. Indeed, in recent years the concept of professionalism has come under fire. Schon describes it this way:

> The crisis of confidence in the professions, and perhaps also the decline in professional self-image, seems to be rooted in a growing skepticism about professional effectiveness in the larger sense, a skeptical reassessment of the professions' actual contribution to society's well-being through the delivery of competent services based on special knowledge. (13)

One source of uncertainty about professional effectiveness is the increasing complexity of many professional tasks. Faced with ambiguity, uniqueness, instability, and value conflict in their tasks, many professionals, as well as those they serve, have developed competing views of the professional role. As Graff has documented, English studies has not been exempt from this complexity. Indeed, uncertainties seem to have plagued English studies from its earliest years. Not coincidentally, the development of English studies as an academic subject coincided with the development both of professionalism and of universities in this country. Graff does not include composition studies in his discussion, and composition's history is, of course, different from that of literature. The current emphasis upon professionalism in composition studies does, however, suggest that professionalism has become a force in our field. And, given the questions raised about the nature of professionalism as well as the connection between positivism and professionalism, we should consider whether this is really a productive direction for composition studies.

A more productive direction might be for composition studies to celebrate its unique qualities, to eschew the professionalism that defines itself in positivist terms, and to embrace an epistemology

consonant with the goals of teacher research. The kind of professionalism exemplified by teacher-researchers suggests an alternative to
the positivist model. Teacher-researchers create knowledge without
making absolutist claims for it. In so doing, they reduce the hierarchy
and exclusion that often characterize professionalism.

An epistemology more consonant with the goals of teacher research
might begin by describing teacher research as a form of cultural
studies. This term, the subject of continuing elaboration, has been
appropriated by literary theory, but, tied as it is to the Arnoldian
view of culture as an aesthetic category, literary theory faces the task
of trying to push beyond this aesthetic definition to what Raymond
Williams calls "a constitutive process, creating specific and different
ways of life" (19). Composition studies faces no such difficulty, and its
interdisciplinary nature offers a unique advantage. The administrative
convenience of locating composition studies in English departments
does not obviate composition's intellectual connections to other disciplines in both the humanities and social sciences, and these connections facilitate thinking about specific and different ways of life.
Heath's description of work done in Roadville and Trackton demonstrates how teacher research functions as a form of cultural studies.
With Heath's help, teachers learned to build a two-way channel
between community and classroom.

> Many of these teachers' ideas for building school skills on
> home skills and ways of talking were simply imaginative,
> intuitive teaching strategies. But many were also backed
> by some social science theory and descriptive facts about
> their own and their students' backgrounds and the uses
> of oral and written language in different communities.
> (293)

Because it gives language a central place, has interdisciplinary connections, and privileges many kinds of texts, composition studies is
uniquely qualified to undertake projects in cultural studies, and
teacher research offers a methodology for enacting this kind of study.
Liberated from the divisions created by positivism and professionalism, scholars in composition can investigate how the language of
various communities—disciplinary communities, work communities,
social communities—is constituted and how the classroom can connect with that language. Like all academic subjects, composition
studies incorporates multiple factions and divisions—we can call
them subcommunities. These communities can likewise come under

investigation in teacher research projects. Just as Graff recommended that the points of conflict and division in literary study become objects of investigation, so I propose that composition studies scrutinize the various communities within and adjacent to itself. Thus, if we conceive of composition programs as centers of teacher research, research based on a socially constructed epistemology and freed from the hierarchies of professionalism, we can transform the theory-practice division into theorizing about practice and practicing theory.

9

A Balanced Survey Course in Writing

Richard Lloyd-Jones

Creating a writing course is an ultimate balancing act. The theoretical understanding of writing and learning weighs against the practical limits of individual students in a particular place at a particular time with a particular teacher. It is, in fact, a rhetorical situation and inevitably unique. Rhetoric (as the ancient Greeks told us) is primarily a practical art, and we teachers must make practical decisions about our art for every class and student.

The first practical step is to say to the teacher, "Know thyself." At least, know the role one is required to play. The teacher should be first a master writer, a person suitable for imitation. But one rarely finds a master of all modes, and anyway "master writer" is not exactly the complete role for a modeling teacher. The academic article writer is not necessarily a competent essayist, nor a technical writer, nor a poet, nor a political speech writer. Nor even an adequate teacher of writing. A teacher/coach balances great competence in one kind of writing with passable awareness in many areas—and something else.

One may write well and know about one's own writing processes, and about processes generally, yet for a teacher/coach the problem is to translate such knowledge so that it can affect the writing of particular students not at all like the teacher. As a writer one is at most a slant-wise model for student writers. Even the best teachers of writing are limited, and must play to their strengths while compensating for their weaknesses. So it is for teachers of any subject, but coaches can't hide behind the lecture barriers of inert knowledge. They must re-earn their credentials as writers with the practical decisions made in each class session.

The writing teacher is chiefly a coach, not a grader or a didact. Most classes should approximate the editorial conference with a student text before the group, the teacher presiding and contributing but primarily drawing out reactions from others. The person setting the agenda has great power, of course, and should use it, but the point is constantly to demonstrate the transactional nature of writing and reading.

I prefer not to grade individual papers because concentrating on the high-level abstraction of value represented in a grade undermines the role of supportive coach and reminds everyone of the institutional role of credit giver. That role is part of the situation, and the students never wholly forget. The person who gives the ultimate grade must try to be fair within the institutional system, but a preoccupation with defending a grade draws attention from the real goals of the course. In some ways a teacher is fortunate if credit depends on the rating of external observers so that students and teacher are clearly allied in developing the students' abilities. That is not to say, however, that the outside rating is more sound. A sensible grade depends upon sustained observation in varied situations.

The exact role a teacher plays depends on the class, so to limit my generalizations and illustrations properly I will allude to a course I taught in the spring of 1989. Whatever elegant theories may guide my decisions, in actual situations one must balance ideal neatness with actual messiness. I've therefore added as an appendix an abridged version of my challenges to the class.

The tasks are variations of what I often suggest at this level, and I believe the principles illustrated can govern survey courses for students of many kinds. The goal is to enhance versatility by sampling a broad range of rhetorical situations. With less able classes I spend more time in each area, playing more variations on each theme. In advanced classes I press more toward the theoretical issues illustrated by each task. I also vary the surface situations according to the interests of the students and what issues are current in the news, or simply how the schedule of holidays and weekends affects the available time.

In that spring at my research university I accepted into my elective class twenty juniors and seniors, two above the official maximum, because I assumed that I'd have 10 percent drop when they understood the rules of the game I expected to play. None dropped. All had completed the freshman course, most with high grades. About a third of the students were majoring in English and planning to enter law school or teaching. Most of the others came from the social sciences; a few were majoring in hard sciences or other humanities areas. At least half had interrupted their college work since being graduated from high school and so were slightly older than traditional students. Several were married; several seniors were on the job market. The main anomaly was that only one was male; usually I have a gender balance. The students were notably conscientious, reasonably venturesome, and socially adept. These traits affected the class sessions more than they altered the nature of the suggested tasks.

As is my wont, I began the semester by getting acquainted and exemplifying our modes of classroom inquiry. Since class members always begin as strangers but within similar contexts are quite similar, my opening gambits are standard. Half of the the first session goes to official chores, and the other half is devoted to the students writing in a single sentence some view of their world. This time I asked them to represent in what sense they were "Writers." I dittoed the sentences for our discussion in our second session. About a third implied they wrote to satisfy themselves, about a third gave some transactional justification, and the rest made some formal claim—"I write poetry" or "I write academic papers." No one claimed to be a writer by virtue of writing letters home, but several indicated the importance of being understood by others. Several were nervous about being a "Writer"—that was too demanding a role—and most made ritually modest disclaimers about the limits of their skill. As a class we noted the implications of different emphases, described the voices of individual writers suggested even in one sentence, and commented on what qualities of writing made us pay attention. We conscientiously avoided "good" or "bad," concentrating instead on what the text revealed.

The first sessions of any of my classes are devoted to building a community of scholars, a goodly fellowship of people helping each other. Since here the students all revealed their attitudes toward writing, we could make overt many of their tacit crippling preconceptions about language, but the primary effort is to build trust in each other. I cannot imagine a serious study of language that is not based in bringing minds together. Not only do we in my writing classes spend most of each day in conversations about particular pieces of writing, we occasionally divide into groups of three or four for more intimate discussions, and I distribute a class phone book to encourage people to work together. Every paper has a real audience of student peers even when the writing is nominally directed to someone else; when we deal with external audiences, the group collaborates on solutions to the writing problem and thus shares in negotiating the meanings.

Beyond these practical efforts to develop a classroom community, my organizing strategy for a survey course is to begin with expressive writing (in the Britton sense) and to edge into more evidently transactional tasks. We finish off with games designed to explore language itself. When Britton uses the terms *expressive* and *transactional* to identify the functions of language, he is building on the idea that languages are symbolic representations within a society. Language always represents something other than itself—that is, it expresses someone's sense of reality—and always serves to establish relationships among the people who use it, serves to act across the gaps that separate human personalities. In any particular situation one function probably dominates, so it is possible to talk usefully of expressive or transactional speaking or writing. Furthermore, the language itself exists as an entity, so it is possible to talk about it, too. Such talk is the business of linguists and critics of various stripes, but we all qualify as those conscious of our own utterances. This elemental model of language in use offers a plan for a course, but only in practical acts of writing does the course really take shape.

Expressive writing, then, requires the students to find language to represent how they make sense of the external world. In popular parlance this goal is sometimes equated with "spilling one's guts onto paper" because it emphasizes that the sources of knowledge are personal, individual. But that phrase overstates the case. Expressiveness is part of superficially remote prose, too. One is also expressive in ordinary explanations cast in "objective," reportlike language, for these are necessarily interpretations of the writer (or the writer's society). Positivist custom invites the illusion of separation of the writer from the reality, so readers may forget that the writer chooses both the structure and the events to be reported. By contrast, a diary, for example, is manifestly interpretive even though it too contains representations of fact. My first objective is to have students control the knowledge they have acquired firsthand, *personal knowledge* in the sense that Michael Polanyi uses the term.

I start out with narratives of personal experience because each person knows more about these events than can be reported, because the narrative forms are part of everyone's social experience even though the knowledge is primarily tacit, because the skills of narration have rarely been badly muddled in previous classroom experience, and because the information itself tends to bind the community by revealing a common background and establishing a shared world within the class. Asking students to write for each other reinforces the fellowship of the class, to be sure, but in most ways it is writing for an alter ego. When we write in diaries, we also write for an imagined self (although in another age one might have written to balance one's accounts with the deity). The creator-self writes to the critic-self, an alter ego. The class is a fictional external audience, one created by the writer in her or his own image, but modified in class discussion. The early emphasis in the course, thus, is on using language to formulate ideas even though we tend to talk about the personal voice.

For this class the adage I used as a starter in task 2—experience is the best teacher—is one I often use, for it is open-ended and yet evokes a narrative response formed to make a point. Students can write about whatever is close at mind with whatever degree of intimacy they find comfortable. Unlike Walter Pater or some novelists, I seek the fruit of experience more than the experience itself. Even if the writer chooses to be an exhibitionist, primarily showing the self in action, my aim is to reveal how a human shapes events. The expressed narrative facts of the case (to paraphrase the legal formula) demonstrate an abstract principle (make a point, teach a lesson) even if the writer does not make it explicit. An abstraction— the fruit of the experience which gives it shape—is defined by a narrative example, so we can observe the function and relevance of concrete details as they develop the governing idea. This issue of evidence I usually save for later, though, and devote the class discussion to the nature of the narrator, the filter of events. We ponder how some intelligence has sifted through the details of experience, has transformed sensations into meaning. In a broad sense our first classroom concern here is with personality and epistemology, how the narrator controls meaning.

The subsequent narratives in my sequence are built partly in response to classroom discussion but mostly in order to establish contrasting narrative goals. I can vary the nature of the abstract stimulus—experience, crisis, event, confrontation, struggle, and so on—or the time of awareness or the expectations of the audience. In short, I change the narrator's purpose and perception so different events are chosen to tell the "same" story. As a practical matter, this class anticipated the main issues, so I built up a catalogue of four or five stories and spent less time on re-visions of the same events. We even struggled with the problems of meaninglessness, of randomness in reporting events. That derailed us temporarily into discussing essay exams written by hard-laboring students who don't really understand the material at hand. Such students can't give shape to details, interpret them, because they haven't internalized the meaning even though they may have worked conscientiously and sometimes feel underrewarded for their work. I encouraged the digression because it anticipates the later problem of guiding students from firsthand impressions reported in narrative to conventional exposition as a means of organizing knowledge.

When Theodore Baird or some of his Amherst descendants opened with similar abstractions, they were engaging in a Neoplatonic exercise of definition, a different kind of epistemological excursion. You can hear in the background of their sequences a Socratic dialogue. They use writing to explore an ideal conception, as Plato explored the good in the *Euthyphro*. Some of them—William Coles, for example—implicitly accept a classical view that language is the reality rather than a designed map of an aspect of reality. Truth can be discovered by those who explore the language carefully. Others— Walker Gibson comes to mind as one tainted by existentialism—are far more tentative, more concerned with the limits of language and the distortions imposed by the individual will. I go farther in suggesting that the narrator defines the external reality even as that reality defines a self for the narrator. Writers continually seek in a socially created language an equilibrium of meaning negotiated with readers about something external to them. Each time one tells a story, even a formula story or a casual bit of swapping lies, one reveals a tacit commitment to meaning. The fish-that-got-away story implies understanding about social exaggeration and companionship, but it also evokes a view of nature and social order that is not as inevitable as it seems, but is rather the choice of teller and hearer. Both for the sake of a liberal education and a mastery of craft, students gain from making such tacit assumptions overt.

Expressing and assuming a view of reality is ordinarily part of a transaction, even if it is only with oneself. When I begin to shift to a rhetorical concern for audiences in task 8, to affect people clearly different from the writer, I am only edging toward transactional writing. In fact, I am then concerned more with how considering the needs of the audience alters one's own sense of reality, how one reexpresses—re-creates—the world to fit another kind of mind or self with its own needs and purposes. Often the daily newspaper provides parallel examples of how the conventions of reporting reshape events to compete for the attention of bored readers. The campus paper is especially helpful, partly because the writers often depend on formulas to compensate for their lack of understanding of the content and partly because class members sometimes have independent knowledge of the events reported. In tasks 8 and 9 especially, our concern for the audience is couched in terms of invention, purpose, and truth. (Is a textbook simplification "true"? Is it less true than the barely intelligible scholarly article? Is the article "true" if the reader can't understand it?) Still, I also raise the notion that all language is sermonic or persuasive by the fact of its representing a particular person's point of view. Persuasion is inherent in the exemplary nature of expression.

In fact, in this particular class most students did very well writing for those younger than themselves, despite some ambivalence about the moral responsiblity they found implied in the relationship. In a sense they wrote to a memory of themselves, but they had suppressed the degree to which they depended on—welcomed—the guidance of their elders. They found in reworking their initial stories that they left out juicier details (which were perhaps irrelevant anyway) and explained some events they had merely alluded to in earlier versions. Language is not morally neutral, although a few of the hard-science people had learned otherwise, but we did not need existentialism to remind us that both choosing and refusing to choose have consequences. Omissions and explanations change stories, and in several instances make better stories, although just reconsidering the events might do that too. But certainly the results are not the "same."

Writing for authority seemed much more difficult, for most of these students had trouble imagining what a rational and responsible person needs to know. So far, most of them had lived in worlds where managerial decisions were made by others; they had become passive suppliants to order givers or knee-jerk rebels, two sides of a single coin. Most had received school instruction in how to prepare reports or "papers," but they hadn't seen that the conventional forms had any relationship to responsible interpretation of information— or that "responsible" is a complex social relationship. In some ways the "forms" had created such firm categories that students had not considered what purpose was served by various formal decisions. My real shift to transactional writing in this class began when I asked people to talk about jobs that they had held—task 12. In a survey of kinds of writing one needs a bridge from the specific experience of personal interest to general experiences of a social or academic interest, so I seek situations which exemplify an initiation into adult responsibility. The shift from describing a daily personal routine (task 6) to describing a standard operating procedure at work (task 10) is essentially one of accepting the social implications of personal acts by generalizing them. One no longer names actions to define one's own nature but rather explains actions which are socially determined. On the job, actions have manifest public consequences; individuals can be replaced, even as parts are replaced in a machine. To explain a personal routine (such as starting the day before one is really awake) requires organization much like that of the procedure, for the events are grouped within a temporal sequence, but the surface is markedly different in suggesting purpose. Although American routines of waking up are remarkably similar, we have at least the illusion of free choice. In contrast, procedures are determined by public need.

Once I had established the grounds for transactional writing, I ran a series of variations tied to the same base of employment experience to raise questions of how form relates to purpose, but I made an excursion into conflict resolution in tasks 17 to 19. These three efforts allow greater emphasis on social action and lighten the pressure of formal decorum a bit. Sometimes in election years, or when some issue rocks the campus, I suggest more transactions with evident public consequences, persuasion as an act of citizenship. These transactional excursions give me a chance to suggest some more dramatic aspects of responsibility and keep the students' adrenaline flowing.

In this semester's sequence of mundane transactions, the students did quite well in imagining what employees and customers needed to know, less well in taking roles addressing authority. They "hated" writing a letter to recommend one acquaintance over another (task 16) even though in task 14 they had considered carefully sensible standards for judgment. In classes primarily for science or business students, I draw out more explicitly sections of the course dealing with developing specifications or presenting judgmental comparisons. Here we barely tried the methods, so probably some discomfort arose from feeling not competent to judge. Nonetheless, for most of the class these tasks represented a world they expected to enter, albeit a shade unwillingly.

The Peter Pan refusal to accept responsibility for hard decisions was only a classroom whimsy, but few of the students had really considered what a future job might entail. In order to write a paper they had to look up some descriptions of the qualifications and duties expected in jobs they wanted to hold. They didn't have an excess of knowledge that made selection of details the main issue. In describing jobs they had already held, they had to make explicit vaguely perceived standards and duties, and that was startling to some, but they did have the data. Even after having discovered such a pattern for describing "work," they were amazed to recognize how much of their future was hidden under hazy general terms. The form of the description became a template demanding some searching for information.

Employment counseling is a by-product of the task, though, for I am concerned primarily with the writer's obligation to frame statements to fit the needs of others. My classroom writers want to serve their own needs, but they have to recognize that their needs are served only when the broader needs of an audience of strangers are also served. In the early tasks we explore making human contact expressively, slowly divesting the veils of anonymity to make friends through verbally shared experiences. But in the transactional tasks we build sustained although precisely limited relationships within the decorum of highly structured situations. Not friends so much as fellow citizens or employees. The purpose is not so much "to be" as "to do." (Students ordinarily like the first nine tasks of the course and the last six better than these in the middle even though they admit that the midsection is useful. They say they are tired of courses that deny them their own reactions, and they equate the conventionality of transactional language with the petty tyranny of the schoolroom.)

The third section of the course emphasizes language for its own sake and inevitably competes for time, energy, and attention with term papers and exams in other courses. Before my university had a battery of linguistics courses, I sometimes bootlegged a bit of formal linguistics. Later, before we had rhetoric and stylistics for writers, I slipped in that kind of material. Even now I engage such subjects both in the tasks and in discussion, but I emphasize *writerly* questions. The term should be understood as parallel to *painterly* in art. If poets are literally "makers," we are all poets, making lilacs out of dead words. Craft seems to have earned a bad name, perhaps because it is associated with inane formalism, but anyone who has played with blocks or Legos or numbers should have fun stacking up words. Those not majoring in English, although initially frightened by this attitude, in the end report having the most fun because they previously perceived writing—indeed, language—in grim terms.

The issues in each of the final linguistic challenges are externally formal. In the early parts of the course, form emerges from purpose and tacitly understood conventions of social interaction. Our meaning is inextricably tied to form, but we observe and name forms after the fact, when we read and criticize each others' statements. In the later tasks, formal labels and examples are considered before the writing is attempted because the tasks are designed to emphasize writing as an object, a "product," if one must say so. The product is not governed by "the minimum essentials of English," however, but by intentional distortion of language. We aren't coloring between the lines; we are whipping the lines about and blotching color in exciting spots. I ask the students to produce not transparent prose providing direct access to content, but translucent prose, to some extent reminding us that direct access is an illusion, but also distancing both writer and reader from each other and the material. In short, if we think language is as much an entity in communication as "self" and "other person," then we should look at it directly.

In this class no one produced great art, although most claimed to be exhilarated by the effort, and some produced stimulating passages. More important, class members saw themselves as Writers, capable of commanding language as well as reporting experience and serving others. A few may even have fed an embryonic obsession with language. In other semesters I've been more schoolish, exploring the *OED* or observing sexist and racist language or making parodies, but my intent remains to attend to the medium itself, and this group of people seemed ready to roam. They had been earnest, even when being expressive, but after the second or third week they stopped worrying about grades. They had read a lot of papers by others, and had heard class discussions, and knew they belonged in the group. They wanted to show off and try outrageous tricks. "Look, Ma, no hands!" Although the end of the semester revived worries about grades, those worries weren't tied to these tasks. They had already been liberated from the notion that I was looking for "right" answers, but they did have college credentials to consider. Apologetically, though, for they liked being liberated.

This course is now fixed in the language of past experience, although the strategy persists. The balances it required—and didn't always get—seem as definite as the skill of a juggler in a painting. We don't see the painted ball roll on the ground, and we only guess that the ones suspended are meant to move and be caught. Yet this static example gives body to some general points about courses.

Writing imposes obligations of ethical relationships. Trying to balance "truth" and "ability to understand and care" is a conflict of demands. Politicians sometimes lie by telling truth so exactly that hearers are misled. So, too, teaching to serve immediately perceived needs may conflict with the pondering required for lifelong wisdom. The classroom community is not automatically a microcosm of the world, but in a democratic society it ought to model cooperativeness in the context of unequal talents and experience. Civility need not be dishonest, and courage ought not be confused with aggression. One must be as nonjudgmental as a therapist even while exploring the very epitome of judgment making inherent in verbal choice. I can't imagine teaching such a course without having theorized about the medium. Yet in producing text one seems to fly on automatic pilot, looking intently at an idea while words emerge from the corner of one's mouth, just as at night real vision comes to the edge of the eye. Each classroom minute brings a new adaptation.

The appendix, which I have lightly glossed, miscues you to think of this essay as an article, but by now you've discovered that it is like the false cue that teases readers in a detective story. Even the course itself, so definite in outline, is a speculation. My reporting has created it in ways not imagined by the registrants, although fairly close to my intentions. Serendipity affected each session. We used language even as we exercised with it; we analyzed its public existence in and out of the classroom as in the papers. To some extent it was a recurring happening in its particulars even though it emerged over and over from the same broad conception.

Students who are comfortable in a didactic world are sometimes made uneasy by the "vagueness" of such a course. They equate precision with lecture outlines, red marks, and the scores on multiple-choice tests, partly because they have never heard about errors of measurement. Students with checkered academic records—often with marginal grade point averages—sometimes blossom, but they also sometimes deceive themselves by confusing freedom with inaction. Some students always imagine that given one more day they'll find the "right" paper, not recognizing that a paper every time the class meets implies, contrary to Francis Bacon, that readiness is a virtue of writing as well as of conference. The descent to Avernus is always easy, so returning responsibility for one's actions to students guarantees some lapses. Even Milton conceded that free choice opens the way to sin.

But it is not amiss to add a dash of moral coercion to help solidify a student's fantasy of eloquence. A coach may express sadness, disappointment. A noble mentor may stand betrayed by a wayward worshipper. Guilt moves more writers than does fear of punishment, for writing is finally evidence of a social relationship more than it is a product. In our language is our character in both classical and modern senses, so in writing we can realize who we are and who they are. That does not really promise a tidy course.

Appendix 9–1: Abridged Schedule of Assignments

Task 1 (in class): You have registered for a class in "writing" that presumes you have previous experience and competence as a "Writer." In one sentence tell us in what sense you are now a "Writer."

Task 2: "Experience is the best teacher." So goes the adage. Write for us (the class) an account of a relatively recent experience important to you. [Through task 20 the assignments were given in written form at the end of the hour while new papers were handed in and old ones picked up.]

Task 3: Tell us about another experience, but this time choose one farther in the past, one that now has a markedly different meaning to you from what it did at the time.

Task 4: Although we recall some events because they seem to teach us something, others stand out because they represent turning points, crises, in our lives. To be sure, we probably learn from our crises, but the term implies a different value set on the events. Tell us about a crisis in your life, not necessarily earthshaking, but still important to you.

Task 5: When we are working out relationships with other people, we tend to tell stories that are dramatic or have some evident thesis. We shape the specific events with some sense of "story" that unveils part of our value system and invites a reader (listener) to join in our community. Yet most of our days are governed by forms we don't usually consider either experiences or crises. Habit? Routine? Custom? Ritual? One might describe them as offering the order that is our stay against the chaos of novelty, or perhaps the relief of being supported by an automatic pilot. Write for us an account of one of your routines so that we will understand what it is and how it serves you.

Task 6: Routines are rarely exciting, but they give us order, and are closely related to standard operating procedures, the systems that govern most of our "business" activities. But most of us also experience nonexciting times when we find ourselves "at loose ends." Events occur and occupy time, but they seem to have little meaning for us even as habits. Tell us about a series of events you found to be in this way "meaningless."

Task 7: Let's stop to recapitulate a bit. You have had four tasks that dealt with events in sequences. In a loose sense all are narratives and based on "real" events. On the basis of what you recall of your own mental processes, tell us how you decided what events to report and what to ignore. Especially note how you decided what were the first and last events of the series (not necessarily the same as how you started or ended your paper). In short, distinguish what gave the papers their forms.

Task 8: Many of you observed how your sense of audience affected your choices of details to be included in a paper. Let's pursue that observation a bit. Recast any of your four sequences for an audience of, say, thirteen-year-olds.

Task 9: Recast the events of one of the four earlier tasks for an audience standing as a "parent" in relation to the events. Although you may in fact write for a parent, I'm using the term metaphorically to stand for a person in authority: a boss, the dean, the sheriff, the landlord, anyone who might stand as judge of the events you described. You undoubtedly know the facts better than the audience does; that is why you write. But the readers have a social role implying responsibility for a decision about the meaning of events. Why do they need to know? How much?

Task 10: Let's shift our efforts to "standard operating procedures." We are still talking about repeated actions in sequence, but we move up a step in abstractness and our purposes are more evidently transactional. The procedures are not idiosyncratic, but are tied to a situation or job. "This is how we open the store" or "this is how we write a term paper" or even—by another little leap to "process" talk—"this is how a computer works." Ordinarily we "teach" about procedures and processes. For this task explain to us a procedure you've done many times and understand well.

Task 11: Prepare an efficient set of directions. Your purpose is to get the job done right, whether or not the person understands. Consider how little "understanding" you care to have when you assemble a toy or a piece of furniture from a kit. For that matter, many of us drive cars or use computers without much desire to understand the machines. People who use recipes rarely care much about chemical reactions in preparing food. What systems of language—layouts, diagrams, photographs, syntax, outline coding—can help? How should information be ordered? Grouped? Emphasized?

Task 12: Most of us look for situations in which we can be "responsible." We agree to perform a variety of tasks and be responsible for the outcomes. One name for such a situation is "holding a job," although the idea is broader than that. Tell us about a job you held so that we'll know precisely what it was and what was expected of you. You might observe that although jobs require actions, and we need to know what they are, usually they are defined by outcomes, the objects or acts for which you are responsible.

Task 13: Drawing on your experience of the job, argue the case that it would be a good choice for a person in circumstances like yours at the time. Write to the likely candidates for such a job and (if appropriate) to the people (parents, perhaps) responsible for them. Note that although you need to describe the job somewhat in order to anchor the argument, you really need to reveal the basis on which you'd judge a job to be "good."

Task 14: Job candidates also are judged. Some standards are absolute. For example, to drive a delivery truck, you must have a valid license; no collection of other virtues can make up for the lack. Each test renders a simple yes-or-no answer, although it is sometimes difficult to decide what is really minimal. (For example, must a firefighter be male?) Relative standards are much more complicated because you must balance the importance of various standards, the degrees of difference between the items being compared, and the validity of your means of measurement. Explain the standards an employer (in the broad sense) would have to use in choosing a person for the job you described. You'll probably want to separate the absolute and relative standards and indicate how to value the relative ones. Also, you ought to indicate what evidence should be used to judge whether the standards had been met.

Task 15: Verbal languages are often blended with graphic ones. Every paper has a visual dimension that is part of the communication. Layout is always an issue, but illustrations, subheadings, bindings, and the like also send messages. Observe the effect of a handwritten note added to a perfectly typed letter. Imagine how you'd convey information about the job you've been discussing to possible candidates. Prepare a poster, display ad, general notice, or whatever seems appropriate to reach the largest audience of appropriate candidates for the job.

Task 16: Suppose two of your acquaintances apply and the person responsible for the hiring asks you to write a letter explaining which one you'd choose. Write the letter, remembering that you owe your honest opinion both to the employer and your acquaintances.

Task 17: Sputtering about how somebody caused you trouble may be a harmless way to vent a little spleen and amuse one's friends. Writing about such problems often externalizes our irritations and thus lets us control them. Write to us about a (recent) situation in which you were injured, frustrated, bothered, delayed, cheated, or otherwise done wrong by another human being. The University's bureaucracy doubtless offers lots of possibilities, but you needn't feel limited to that. For this task, don't worry about being fair; we'll understand. Just have fun getting it out of your system by concentrating on your feelings.

Task 18: Describe the event that set off your diatribe from the point of view of the person who caused the fuss. This time try to capture what probably was that person's sense of the situation.

Task 19: Keeping in mind both your righteous anger and your awareness of the other person's problem, propose to that person (or that person's boss) a procedure to redress the wrong or prevent similar events in the future. You'll note that this requires you to enlarge your perspective, to redefine the events, in terms of a more inclusive situation.

Task 20: Cast your mind five years beyond your final academic degree to the job you'd like to hold. Describe your dream so that we understand what the job requires, what would draw you there, and what credentials you would have to possess to tempt a personnel committee to invite you in. You'll note that in many ways this is a reprise of the problems in tasks 12 through 15, but here it implies planning rather than recollection.

Task 21: Prepare a letter of application (with a resume) for the job you described in task 20. To cover the gaps of five years or so, supply as though accomplished the achievements you know you'll have to have. (Stay moderately close to probability.) You might note that this is specialized persuasion, so pay particular attention to what the reader is going to need to know in order to make good absolute and relative judgments. [We discussed examples of writing required in tasks 21 to 25 in class before students went out to try their own. These tasks were presented in a single packet with suggested due dates but with general permission to students to pace the material to fit their other obligations.]

Task 22: Each of the remaining tasks involves some play with language, but play is serious business for humans. Still, try to put your inhibitions to rest and have some fun. I won't growl if the results are a bit overdrawn. Playfulness is a bit hard to command. This task and the next one deal with metaphor. First, write down the names of five common things within your range of vision. Second, note what idea each suggests to you other than itself (e.g., a dog might suggest loyalty, or servility, or playfulness). Third, choose one of the suggestions for one of the items as a base for your expression of a belief or value you think worthy of exploration. That is, explore the idea by means of exploring the original object.

Task 23: This time act as a teacher by means of a metaphor. Explain a subject you know and care about by means of a single extended metaphor, or a tissue of metaphors, so that the reader is led to understanding (and perhaps emotional acceptance) of the idea by reference to something else. In a sense, task 22 encourages you to understand an idea you can't otherwise quite express, but task 23 is based on the premise that you are already an expert, though your readers are not, so you are drawing on your readers' sensory experience in order to explain to them your understanding. The first effort is exploratory for you; the second is didactic for you, although probably exploratory for your readers. In fact, neither pattern is "pure." Any metaphor has the capacity to suggest nuances even on familiar topics, just as any metaphor is controlled by a base of prior knowledge.

Task 24: Here is an experiment with syntax and rhythm, an effort to push language to its limits. Each will seem odd, but try to make an idea intelligible at least and perhaps effective. First, without using any verbs or verbals tell about something you recently did. Second, tell us the same story with generally the same details in a single, highly articulated sentence. Third, tell us the same story without using any adjectives or adverbs.

Task 25: Essay any topic you like by means of verbal irony. I've used the word "essay" in a somewhat peculiar way to emphasize that I don't mean the word as it appears in the phrase "essay exam." I don't object to your also using situational or dramatic irony, but I'd like you to emphasize saying one thing while you mean us to interpret something different—and, of course, providing us with cues to reassure us that you are ironic, not crazy.

Task 26 (due during final week): Prepare two copies of your description of what you've written this semester. Note what qualities you especially liked and what you'd like to work on during the next few months. Please include your papers as an appendix (I want to reread them as a complete package), but also cite examples in enough detail that I'll understand your points now and again next year. I will keep one of the copies in my file along with a copy of my reaction to your comment so that if you ask me to serve as a reference for you, you'll know what I will say and I will have enough detail to write you a decent letter. The originals of all these documents and your course grade will be ready for you to pick up at my office in a few days. I hope that you will find this exercise useful enough in setting your own goals that you'll want to repeat it every few months, but for now recognize that I'm asking your help in reporting a course grade to the Registrar, so don't be falsely modest or blandly unaware.

10

Designing for Change in a Writing-Across-the-Curriculum Program

Richard Young

I

As a friend of mine, a professor of nuclear engineering, used to say, the half-life of an educational program is about five years. He was right, of course, about the inevitability of decay, but his metaphor suggests a measured decline that is not borne out by experience. Biological metaphors like birth, maturity, and aging are more accurate when applied to educational programs, since they suggest more variation in the process of growing old, and more surprises. They also suggest the possibility of intelligent behavior and thus of deferring the inevitable. However, the hard fact remains that programs decline, sometimes astonishingly fast. When a program begins to show signs of terminal illness or senility, an ad hoc committee starts looking around hopefully for parents with better genes and drawing up plans for educational euthanasia, a necessary though unpleasant and wasteful process.

So when I was asked to develop a four-year, writing-across-the-curriculum (WAC) program at Carnegie Mellon University, I began considering whether there might be a way if not to stop the birth-to-death cycle, at least to slow it significantly. If images of decay prompted my inquiry, evolution eventually became its controlling metaphor. I asked myself whether there might be a way of developing a self-renewing educational program: that is, a program that would be able to adapt readily to new conditions, assimilate innovations in the discipline, curb proposals for change that threaten to jeopardize the program, improve itself by solving its own problems, and so on— in general, a program that could and would change in ways roughly analogous to evolution in the biological world. My immediate, practical goal was a way of developing a WAC program that would be both effective and sustainable.

In what follows, I want first to characterize conventional program development, then to argue that it is an inappropriate process for developing WAC programs, and finally to describe an alternative process being worked out at Carnegie Mellon University that seems to me to be more appropriate to the task at hand.

II

What characterizes the conventional process of program development? If we look at it on a very abstract level, we see that it is essentially a teleological process.[1] This implies that there is a design that is expected to be realized at the end of the process, something like a blueprint for a building, though the blueprint is probably too detailed and rigid to serve as a close analogy to the designs we start with in program planning. Another characteristic of teleological processes is that they normally include some surprises as they are carried out; as one tries to implement the design, to move from idea to actuality, the unanticipated intrudes and must be accommodated. Hence, unlike a mechanical process, the steps cannot be completely specified in advance. Thus, neither the steps of the process nor its results are entirely predictable.

But the process is intensely purposeful: the initial design provides the primary principle of selection for the steps of the process as well as a description of the intended outcome. The success or failure of teleological processes can be judged by the extent to which the original design is fully realized in the outcome, that is, by the extent to which the purpose has been achieved. Typically, once the design has been realized, control processes are established to maintain the actualized design against pressures for change. In teleological processes, then, a great deal depends on the adequacy of the design, since it shapes both the steps in the process and the outcome and since it is the basis for the new organization that those overseeing the development seek to sustain. Because the success of a teleological process depends so heavily on the quality of the initial design (its clarity, coherence, feasibility), it follows that in the absence of a strong design the outcome of the process is questionable. I want to argue that this conventional—that is, teleological—approach to program development appears to be ill-suited to WAC programs, since the precondition of a strong design is difficult to meet. Why is this so?

III

The characteristic of WAC most telling for program development is that it is, broadly speaking, unprecedented; by that I mean that it is new and that it is different in significant ways from the tradition of writing instruction that it seeks to displace. To say this is to say that we lack the well-elaborated, time-tested designs so important when using conventional planning methods. It is not that effective program development is impossible without strong designs. However, it is likely to require a great deal more luck, hard work, knowledge, and imagination than is required when we develop programs of a more familiar sort; and the risk of failure is higher. That is so any time one tries to create something new; results are always more predictable and easier to achieve when we imitate than when we depart significantly from precedent.

Since it is an important assumption in my argument, let me clarify further what I mean by WAC's being "unprecedented." To begin with, the principles on which WAC programs are being built are quite different from those that underpin traditional composition programs. For example, in a survey of 194 WAC programs, C. W. Griffin observes that "most have something in common—the premises on which they are based" (402). He lists three:

1) Writing skills must be practiced and reinforced throughout the curriculum, otherwise they will atrophy, no matter how well they are taught in the beginning. . . .

2) To write is to learn. . . .
3) Since written discourse is central to a university education, the responsibility for the quality of student writing is a university-wide one. (402–3)

None of these principles has characterized traditional composition
programs, where the cultivation of writing skills is the responsibility
of the English department and concentrated in the freshman year and
where the written language tends to be seen as a means for recording
what has been learned rather than as a heuristic activity that fosters
learning. We should note that Griffin's list is descriptive and not
intended to provide a comprehensive statement of the theoretical
underpinnings of WAC programs. Finding such a statement, however, is difficult. As James Kinneavy has remarked, "There have been
few explicit, comprehensive and substantial statements on the theoretical foundations which have underpinned the many programs [de-
veloped in this country]" ("Writing" [1987] 368). Those working
on WAC seem to be clarifying and elaborating their assumptions as
they go along.

This absence of clarity and elaboration can create serious problems
for the program developer. For example, in "Defining Writing Across
the Curriculum" Susan McLeod notes the pervasive and sometimes
serious misunderstandings about WAC among administrators and
faculty. Deborah Swanson-Owens's recent article, "Identifying Natural Sources of Resistance: A Case Study of Implementing Writing
Across the Curriculum," points to a similar conclusion. In a project
that entailed helping high school teachers use WAC methods, she at
first found apparent agreement on goals and methods, but subsequent
probing revealed disagreements over beliefs about the nature of writing, teaching, and learning so fundamental as to subvert communication between her and the participants. For example, she notes that
the source of new knowledge

> is defined differently by each of the participants in this
> writing project, a difference that affects the way each views
> writing as an instructional tool. Jack believes meaning and
> thus the source of new knowledge resides in the text. For
> Naomi new knowledge develops from new experiences,
> experiences which are generated and monitored by the
> teacher. (91)

Working out of the WAC principle that writing can stimulate discovery, Swanson-Owens, however, "[considered] the students as much a source of new knowledge as the materials and activities themselves. . . . [She] felt that the writing tasks should provide less structure for and ask for more personal analysis from the students— that freedom to generate meaning rather than reproduce it would encourage students to use more complex thinking skills and, in the process, generate new knowledge" (91). I suspect that a close examination of the beliefs held by faculty in virtually any WAC training workshop would reveal comparable disagreements.

David Russell, in "Romantics on Writing: Liberal Culture and the Abolition of Composition Courses," chronicles assumptions widely shared in English departments by opponents of writing programs, assumptions that call into question both the possibility of teaching writing and the desirability of making the effort: the assumptions, for example, that writing can be learned but not taught; that the way to develop writing ability is to have students read good literature; that the basic mission of the English department is the teaching of liberal culture through the study of imaginative literature; that the responsibility for writing instruction, defined essentially as instruction in mechanics, lies with the primary and secondary schools; and so on. Though it is an extreme case, one can see in Scott Heller's account of the WAC program at the University of Texas–Austin how such assumptions can intrude disruptively during the process of program development.[2] "If the teaching of writing is to take a full place in the English department and in the university," Russell argues, "the profession must acknowledge the fundamental ideological conflicts which the abolitionists raised, and face their consequences at last" ("Romantics" 146). The articles by Russell, Swanson-Owens, and McLeod all suggest that the theoretical assumptions driving the WAC movement remain to be adequately explored and that they may well prove to be significant sources of conflict and dissension in academic communities where WAC programs are being introduced.

With a few notable exceptions, the WAC program designs discussed in our professional literature are more often plausible speculations about what is likely to work than descriptions of designs that have been tested and refined over years of actual practice. And the existing programs that are serving us as models, even though they themselves have hardly lost the status of experiments, often tell us more about what not to do than about what is demonstrably effective. For example, in an often-cited article Kinneavy describes two general program designs—designs that have been adopted in many of the most influential programs in the country: "the individual subject approach," in which instruction in writing becomes the responsibility of the various departments, and "the centralized generic system," in which the responsibility for writing instruction is centralized in the English department, although students are asked to write about issues in their various disciplines ("Writing" [1983] 15–17). However, Kinneavy identifies fundamental limitations in both designs and argues for a combination of the two in which the deficiencies of one would be offset by the strengths of the other (17–19), a design that was eventually adopted at the University of Texas–Austin.

Unfortunately, the results at Texas have been disastrous, as the title of Heller's report suggests: "Fifty Lecturers Lose Their Jobs in a Dispute over How—and If—Writing Can Be Taught." Whatever the causes of the program's collapse, and there appear to have been several working in combination, the design of the program was surely one of them. I am not implying that the design was unintelligent or that those implementing it were less than competent. Quite the contrary: I cite the Texas case precisely because on paper at least the design was one of the most promising available at the time; and Kinneavy and the others in the rhetoric group then at Texas are clearly among the most competent rhetoricians in the country. The point I am trying to make is that we still lack the experience necessary in order to generalize with confidence about the characteristics of effective WAC designs.

Partly as a result of the Texas experience, Maxine Hairston, in "Some Speculations about the Future of Writing Programs," introduced another complication into discussions of program development—the influence of the institutional environment. The nature of the institution is so crucial a determinant of the sustainability of writing programs, she argues, that they are not likely to work at all in certain kinds of schools: to be specific, the big universities that have specialized faculties and graduate programs. Hairston may be right; but if we take as a general principle of planning that programs should be shaped to fit the institutional environment, then it becomes a bit risky to use one program as a model for another. The better adapted a program is to its environment, the less appropriate it is to copy it in other environments.

Consider also the unusual pedagogical problems that confront WAC planners. For example, it seems axiomatic that if students are to become better writers, the amount of writing they do must be significantly increased and useful feedback on this writing must be

provided. It also seems axiomatic that programs are unlikely to survive
if they require significant increases in faculty work loads and operating
budgets, for such increases quickly erode faculty and administrative
support. WAC program developers find themselves in a situation in
which they must learn how to do more without doing more. Assuming they can find a way out of this dilemma, only one of a number
implicit in WAC programs, consider the problem of persuading the
faculty and administration that they do in fact know a way out.
Pedagogical problems such as this one quickly become political problems, particularly when start-up money disappears and faculty altru-
ism begins to erode (e.g., Kalmbach). Such problems do not appear
to be insurmountable, but they are problems that program developers
have not normally had to face when planning programs in areas where
there is a tradition of workable precedents to draw on.

The process for developing a WAC program also brings with
it the same organizational, political, and economic problems that
accompany the development of more traditional programs, only in
much more difficult forms. Any program must be housed somewhere
within the institutional structure, inevitable disagreements among
those affected by it must be reconciled, new funds must be found to
get it started and then keep it running, and so on. More traditional
programs are normally proposed by and housed in well-established
academic departments. In contrast, WAC programs often operate
outside the departmental structure and may be housed in any number
of locations in the institution—the dean's office, the president's office,
the writing center, or elsewhere (e.g., Blair; L. Smith). Though
operating outside the departmental system can have advantages, it can
also make the program more vulnerable to criticism and withdrawal of
support. Unlike more traditional programs developed within academic departments, WAC programs are frequently the products of
ad hoc, multidisciplinary groups, each member of which has his or
her own agenda (e.g., Glick). Furthermore, because WAC offers a
promising way of addressing the difficult and widely acknowledged
problems associated with the cultivation of literacy, many WAC
programs have been able to attract special grants from the school
administration or from outside sources, from foundations, government agencies, and corporations. However, the eventual transition
from support by often substantial grants to support by the general
operating budget of some unit within the institution is unlikely to
be easy. Although organizational, political, and economic problems
have not received a great deal of attention in the WAC literature,

they may have as much bearing on whether a program design can be implemented and sustained as any of the other issues mentioned above. It would be a mistake to treat them as though they were peripheral matters to be dealt with after the real business of program development has been accomplished. As Gesa Kirsch points out, sustainable programs must be not only educationally sound but institutionally sound as well (55).

I do not mean to imply that there are no effective programs among the hundreds throughout the country. I am arguing that developing WAC programs that will last is a task that is both unfamiliar and exceptionally difficult, more difficult perhaps than many of us involved with such programs supposed when we committed ourselves to the enterprise. McLeod observes that WAC means deep change—"change in the structure of writing programs, change in the university curriculum, change in faculty behavior in the classroom. At its best, WAC means a change in the entire educational process at the university level" (23–24). Change of that magnitude is infrequent, and it is hard to achieve and to maintain against conservative pressures, as recent historical studies remind us. In a discussion of programs at Colgate and the University of California at Berkeley that are analogous to present-day WAC programs, Russell argues that they

> failed not because they lacked substance, but because they could not overcome the very obstacles which WAC programs are facing today. As Toby Fulwiler, Richard Lanham and others have recently pointed out, cross-curricular writing instruction goes against the grain of the modern university, with its research orientation, specialized elective curriculum, and insular departmental structure—all of which make it extremely difficult to change faculty attitudes toward writing instruction. Despite strong administrative support and an enthusiastic core of faculty members, the Colgate and Berkeley programs were unable to integrate writing into the organizational structure of the university to the extent that cross-curricular instruction became self-sustaining, independent of the dynamic personalities who began the programs. ("Writing" 184–85)

Russell is probably right that if WAC programs are to be sustainable, they must be integrated into the structure and routine practices of the institution. "WAC programs must be woven so tightly into the fabric of the institution as to resist the subtle unraveling effect of academic politics" ("Writing" 191). But how one goes about doing this is unclear.

IV

What do we do, then, as program planners when we're not wholly sure we know what we are doing? Because of the difficulty of the task and the limitations of our theoretical and practical knowledge, planning for continuing, adaptive change in WAC programs—evolution, if you will—appears to be worth considering. Rather than assuming that we know how to design a program that will work as we want it to, and continue to work well for the foreseeable future, those of us working on the WAC program at CMU have tried to make a virtue of change, to acknowledge that the unanticipated and unanticipatable will have a much greater influence than is normally the case in program development where the assumptions are better understood, the designs have successful precedents, and the process for implementing them is better established. Keeping the design fluid, beginning with the assumption that it will evolve, is an acknowledgment that there is much that we do not know that we need to know.

As with teleological processes, evolutionary processes entail selection from among a number of possible choices as the processes are carried out; but unlike them the selection is dictated not by the original design but by changes in the ecological system, which may well be unanticipatable. In the case of academic organizations, such changes might include new ideas in the discipline, new faculty with different competencies, changes in social needs, changes in institutional resources, new administrations with new agendas, and so on. If a change establishes itself in the organization, it reverberates through the system, producing other changes and, hence, a kind of growth in the system and a new equilibrium. This new equilibrium may then be altered as other changes emerge, so that the organization grows, in complexity and sophistication if not in size, through a series of relatively stable states.

One might object that though teleological and evolutionary processes are sharply distinct in theory, they are much less so in actual program planning, and hence that the notion of evolutionary planning has no practical value. After all, developing a program is of necessity teleological since there is always a director making choices guided by a sense of purpose, no matter how general. Furthermore, although in theory teleological processes develop toward a final stable state, most if not all programs change over time in response to changes in their environments. Even granting that human behavior will always be less tidy than our theories about it, a question remains whether, practically speaking, there is such a thing as evolutionary program planning, or whether we are just talking about a highly self-conscious kind of teleological planning that is especially responsive to the considerable uncertainties found in the theory and practice of WAC.

I would like to argue that the notion of evolution can have value for the program planner if it is treated as a metaphor that guides thinking about program development: that is, if its heuristic potential is exploited during the development process. For example, it has encouraged those of us involved in WAC at CMU to regard the development of the program as open-ended, rather than as something that can be completed and then simply maintained. As I will discuss in a moment, it has led us to build into the program design several ways of getting feedback on all features of the program, a prerequisite for intelligent change. It has also led us to give the organizational design for the program (see appendix 10-1) a much less important role than comparable designs of programs described in WAC litera-ture. For us the design has been a statement (a partial one since it says nothing about theoretical principles or pedagogy) of where we have started in developing the program, but not where we will end, even though at the moment the design seems to us to be well thought out.

The metaphor of evolution has also led us to be more opportunistic about program development. The choices we make as the program develops are dictated as much by unanticipated possibilities as by the initial design. For example, a chance meeting with a member of the biology department who became interested in our ideas led us to spend a year developing and observing a simplified, small-scale ver-sion of the program in a single biology course rather than trying to implement the program on a larger scale, as had been our original intention; we saw this as a good way of testing out some of our ideas in a low-risk situation. This project is part of a continuing effort to shape new versions of the program, exploiting opportunities that promise to make it stronger and better adapted to its context. The metaphor also encourages us to regard emerging problems as points at which the program can be developed rather than as failures on our part or perverse efforts on the part of others to subvert the program; this attitude toward problems is not always easy to maintain, but it is on the whole salutary and practical. And the metaphor is helping us to move slowly—evolution rather than revolution—and to be content with moving slowly; for the changes we seek are not shallow and sharply limited but instead go deep and pervade the institution. As Russell observes, "WAC programs require patience. Ten—or thirty—years may not be enough to change century-old university priorities and classroom practices" ("Writing" 191). A good deal of the value of the metaphor, then, is the effect that it has on our attitudes as we develop the program.

What is stable and persistent over time in our program is not the organizational design and the pedagogical methods characteristic of WAC, but a set of assumptions about language and language use. The assumptions in the CMU program are not markedly different from those traditionally associated with the WAC movement; the most important ones are, baldly put, (a) that language is a kind of behavior, more specifically a kind of symbolic action; (b) that a language act is a composite of form and meaning; and (c) that language behavior occurs in a context and is responsive to it. Though the assumptions persist, the way they are manifested in the program will undoubtedly change over time as a result of more experience, new research, shifts in educational values, changing social needs, faculty with new competencies, and so on.

How does the CMU program invite constructive change? So far, four principles have informed our efforts to implement this conception of program development:

1. The program is to grow incrementally through a series of stable phases.
2. It is to be faculty-centered rather than curriculum-centered or student-centered.
3. The program is to be informed by relevant ongoing research.
4. The program and its components are to be subject to regular, formal evaluation.

None of these principles is new to WAC; most have been used before in one program or another. What is perhaps new is their collective function—that of providing regular, reliable, and diverse feedback about the adequacy of all aspects of the program and thus a rational basis for change. Each principle has a part in cultivating a critical self-consciousness among those involved with the program; we hope that together they will foster a kind of ongoing, systematic groping for more effective ways of conducting the program. In addition to creating a more sustainable educational program, they will also, we hope, be a way of exploring the theoretical assumptions that underlie the WAC movement and their implications for education.

1. *Phased development.* The CMU program is being developed, with all deliberate slowness, in a series of phases which with time become more complex in their assumptions and methods and, in the early phases at least, more inclusive in the number of faculty and students involved. Each phase is a relatively stable resting place, with modifications and elaborations suggested by the experience of those directly involved in the program and by research on the effectiveness of proposed methods. Once a phase is well established, we can assess what we have learned to that point, make whatever changes seem desirable, and begin planning for the next phase, the assumption being that our growing knowledge may well lead us in unanticipated directions.

The first phase of the CMU program has had two goals: (a) to develop a general plan that would exploit the strengths of the CMU environment and avoid the problems that have become apparent in several programs elsewhere and (b) to cultivate a group of faculty interested in working on WAC projects. In addition to numerous meetings with faculty and administrators where we have tried out our ideas, we have conducted several projects designed to study and evaluate components of the WAC plan. The first phase culminated in a study of various features of the plan in a classroom setting. As I mentioned a moment ago, for the last year a graduate student and I have been working with a biologist in an intensive observational study of what she and her students do with various write-to-learn techniques and collaborative methods that are important parts of our plan. The project has two purposes: first, and most important, to see how well the techniques and methods work in a sharply limited setting before considering them for use on a larger scale; and second, to try to get a better understanding of the rhetoric of biology and thus something of the diversity of contexts we must learn to appreciate and work in. There is no point in trying to initiate a university-wide program if we cannot successfully establish a smaller, simpler version under highly favorable conditions. On the basis of what we learn, we will no doubt make changes in our thinking about the program as a whole and, more particularly, in what we have sketched out for the next phase.

That next phase, for which we have already submitted grant proposals, entails developing the existing computer network at CMU to create a more supportive context for original thinking and writing. The network would make possible the creation of ad hoc intellectual communities that include both faculty and students; admission to such communities would require only a willingness to participate seriously in any of the ongoing dialogues that spring up on campus. The project also includes development of a writing-consulting service that substitutes E-mail for the traditional writing center; an electronic writing center would make it possible to meet the intermittent need for expert guidance on communication problems for the most part as the need arises during the activity of composing.

2. *The faculty as agents of change.* Like the program at Michigan Technological University, ours is teacher-centered rather than curriculum-centered or student-centered, and by and large for the same reasons (Fulwiler and Young, esp. x–xi). The program focuses on faculty development as the primary means of influencing student literacy (rather than on, for example, proficiency tests or curricular requirements). One great advantage of focusing on the faculty is that they can be an easily accessible, articulate, and sophisticated source of information on the effectiveness of the various aspects of the program and on possibilities we had not anticipated. That assumes, of course, that provision is made for active participation by the faculty in planning and implementing program activities and for regular feedback from the faculty on their attitudes toward the program, on what is effective in their classes, on suggestions for improvements, and so forth.

The strongly dialogic nature of the decision-making process is one of the most important features of the program. In the fall of 1987, faculty from the departments of English, history, and psychology participated in a project studying the use of what we called "essential-issue scales" as aids to criticism in small-group collaborative learning.[3] From interviews at the end of the project with the fifteen participating teachers, I found that in the use of both peer evaluation methods and scales there is a very large number of ways one can go wrong and a very small number of ways to be effective. What seemed clear to me about the use of the methods evidently wasn't to the other teachers. Furthermore, I realized that I did not know the answers to many of the questions they raised. The project has led to a closer examination of the conditions for effective use of collaborative learning, to a study of scale design, and to more care in the presentation of both in class and in faculty workshops.

3. *The role of research.* The program is informed by ongoing research in language and education. As we know, writing programs in this country have been for generations rooted in doubtful theory and the beliefs of inappropriately trained faculty. With the emergence of more reliable research and faculty trained to take advantage of it, the profession is in a position to establish programs that are based on more adequate knowledge and that are more responsive to developments in research.

The CMU program is designed not only to make use of existing research that bears on problems in the program, but also to provide what might be called "ad hoc programmatic research": that is, research carried out on campus with the intention of helping the program directors make intelligent decisions. If the basis for making an intelligent choice does not already exist, a research project can be designed to provide it. Jeanette Harris and Christine Hult's "Using a Survey of Writing Assignments to Make Informed Curricular Decisions" illustrates this sort of research, as does the CMU study on collaborative learning and scales mentioned a moment ago. That project grew in part out of research suggesting that the combination of peer evaluation and scaling can be an effective way of providing feedback on student writing (Hillocks 156–68). We were trying to determine, among other things, whether collaborative learning in small groups where critical evaluation is guided by essential-issue scales could serve as an effective alternative to peer tutoring by trained undergraduates. Both are ways of giving students feedback on their writing; both involve students more extensively in their own learning; but the former is a great deal less expensive.

Commenting on research engendered by WAC Programs, Fulwiler remarks that

> teaching writing in English classes or outside of English classes remains more art than science: we still know very little about what happens at the moment of insight, inspiration, or ideation. Nor do we know predictable routes of faithful translation from thought to language, from pen to paper. So in every attempt to "teach" others to teach writing more often and more thoughtfully in their

classes, problems arise with translation, motivation, situation, assumptions, pedagogy, terminology, personality, and turf. At the same time we who started such programs hoping to amplify the lessons of freshman composition soon found that we had stumbled into fertile territory for pedagogical research, faculty development, institutional cohesion, and personal growth. (114)

Fulwiler's strategic translation of problems into opportunities for research is one of the important survival strategies of academic life—metaphorically speaking, a way of turning sows' ears into silk purses, or, more literally, a way of profiting from our mistakes and thus increasing the chance that the programs will survive.

4. *Program evaluation.* In addition to research on questions generated by the program and the focus on faculty participation, formal evaluation of the program and all its components will also provide information necessary for constructive change. (Evaluations will be conducted by the CMU's Center for Teaching, an extension of activities that are already part of the Center's responsibility.) Experience at Michigan Technological University (Young and Fulwiler) and Robert Morris College (Sipple; Sipple and Stenberg), both of which have made substantial efforts to evaluate their programs, has shown that ongoing, carefully planned evaluation provides a number of important benefits. Among these are improvement in the quality of instruction and a salutary feeling among the faculty of being engaged in a common enterprise; but more important from the point of view I have been developing here is that evaluation can provide another basis for rational decision making and constructive change.

Like most teachers of writing, those of us involved in the Robert Morris project[4] assumed that students must believe that writing is valuable if they are to perform well as writers or want to learn to perform well; thus, we were surprised, and initially at least a bit dismayed, to find that students of teachers trained in our workshops sometimes valued writing less than students of faculty who had had no workshop training. The crucial variable appears to have been not particular techniques and methods of writing instruction, but whether the students were convinced that writing mattered to the teacher. The study showed how important it is that teachers *demonstrate* to students that they regard writing as valuable—a simple verity that is often forgotten when teachers enter the classroom. "Demonstrate" here means more than *saying* that writing is important: it means acts such as (1) assigning writing frequently, (2) incorporating writing performance into the final grade even in classes that do not purport to teach writing, and (3) stressing its importance in various ways (e.g., discussing samples of professional prose in class). Since demonstrating to students that writing is valued is relatively easy, the evaluation process may have uncovered a low-cost method for improving student writing. As the investigators remarked,

> *students value writing more as a learning tool when it is assigned frequently and when it is clearly valued by the teacher.* This is perhaps the single most important finding of this study, as it tells us the conditions necessary for a writing-across-the-curriculum program to succeed. (Coppersmith and Garrow 42)

One important function of the program director is to manage constructive change: to exploit new possibilities and to see to it that the program is moving in promising ways, adapting and readapting itself to the new and unanticipated while maintaining the assumptions that drive it. This requires that the director have a more substantial scholarly involvement with the program than has commonly been the case in traditional composition programs, where the director's scholarly interest is often in an entirely different area of English studies. As Richard Bullock observes in "When Administration Becomes Scholarship," if writing programs are to become "dynamic laboratories in which composition theory and composition pedagogy grow together," administration must become a kind of scholarly performance (17–18). It also requires that the program director have the administrative power to initiate changes—another way in which the director of this program differs from the typical director of traditional composition programs (Olson and Moxley). And it requires that the program director maintain a receptive and opportunistic attitude toward change, which may be a good deal harder to find than scholarly competence. This last point is important since the attitude toward change implicit in the metaphor of evolution may finally be more important than particular features of the planning method. Generally speaking, unless the role of the program director changes from the traditional one of low-level administrator of an already established program to that of a much more independent and creative leader, the approach to program development described here probably will not work.

It is not that those of us working on the CMU program have no idea about what an effective WAC program might look like; we have tried to consider our theoretical assumptions carefully, and we have in fact worked out elaborate organizational and pedagogical plans. But since intelligent plans are not the same as successful programs, we are proceeding cautiously. It should be clear, though, that we do not look forward to a fully developed, stable program, at which time change will cease; we see each new phase as something that not only will change but *should* change under the pressure of new knowledge and new opportunities. To our thinking, what is important is not the design of the program but the principles on which it is based and the approach to program planning discussed here.

One long-term result of continuing efforts at adaptation to changes in the academic ecology will be, we hope, not a generic WAC program suitable for imitation throughout the country but, increasingly, a CMU/WAC program; we assume that something analogous would happen at other schools where this approach to planning is used. That is, the approach should foster the development of well-adapted variants whose viability is enhanced because of a continuing sensitivity and responsiveness to changes in context. It may well contribute to that institutional integration that appears to be essential to the sustainability of educational programs. A planning process haunted by the notion of evolution does not guarantee a sustainable program, but it may well increase our chances of developing one.

Notes

1. Teleological processes contrast with three other basic kinds of process: (a) random processes, in which the steps of the process are irrelevant to the outcome, which is, hence, unpredictable; (b) mechanical processes, in which the precise specification of each of the steps produces a predictable outcome; and (c) evolutionary processes, which proceed through an ongoing series of stable stages that are unpredictable and that change as the result of unanticipatable changes in the populations of the ecology, i.e., those changes that compete successfully for survival (Boulding 1–18).

2. These assumptions and opposing ones are also apparent in efforts earlier in the century to develop programs similar to present-day WAC programs (Combies 81–98).

3. An "essential-issue scale" is a variant of the kind of scale de-

scribed by Lloyd-Jones in "Primary Trait Scoring." It has three basic
components: (1) a list of the essential objectives of the assigned
writing task; (2) after each objective, a space for a brief comment;
and (3) a numerical scale (e.g., 1 to 5) for recording an evaluation
of how well the student has mastered the objective. The list is an
effort to identify not all that might be learned by perceptive students,
but what they are supposed to learn from carrying out that particular
task.

   Unlike generic scales such as the one developed by Diederich,
essential-issue scales are ad hoc, a new scale being designed for each
task. Such scales can serve a number of functions, among which is
providing students with guidance as they criticize each other's work
(Hillocks 156–68).

   4. The start-up grant received by Robert Morris College specified
a reciprocal relationship between Robert Morris and Carnegie Mellon. Several CMU faculty and graduate students were to be involved
in the development of the Robert Morris program, the intention
being that ideas and methods developed at CMU would be incorporated into the Robert Morris program and, in turn, that the experience gained there would feed back into the CMU program.

*A*ppendix 10–1: The Components of the CMU Writing-Across-the-Curriculum Program: Their Nature and Functions

1. The University Oversight Committee is composed of faculty from among the active participants in the program. It recommends policy, advises the Program Director, and serves as a link with the various colleges and the administration.

2. The Center for Teaching monitors and evaluates the program and its components, runs faculty training workshops, and advises participating faculty on an ad hoc basis.

3. The English-as-a-Second-Language Program provides English language instruction for foreign students with the goal of more effective participation in regular classes, including courses in the program.

4. The Computer Network Support System provides instructional services to students on demand. In particular, it diagnoses rhetorical and language problems, recommends appropriate ways of solving them, and evaluates learning. It also acquires, maintains, and supervises student use of a software library for first-language instruction. Finally, it encourages and provides the technology for forming ad hoc collaborative learning groups among students and faculty.

5. Strategies for Writing provides instruction for first-year students in the basics of argument, focusing on argument designed for the general educated reader; it also develops the abilities students

need for carrying out assignments in the upper-level Participating Courses.

6. Designated Writing Courses are first- and second-year courses intended for students exempted from Strategies for Writing and are taught by faculty from various disciplines. The courses provide instruction in the basics of argument, focusing on argument designed for readers in particular disciplines; they also develop the abilities students need for carrying out assignments in the upper-level Participating Courses.

7. Participating Courses are third- and fourth-year courses taught by faculty in the various disciplines. It is important to note that the intellectual focus in such courses is on the discipline, where it has always been, rather than on writing. Writing as such is not *taught*; rather, it is regularly *used* as a means of learning the discipline more effectively. The exception to this practice is the case in which the instructor wishes to develop the students' understanding and control of the various rhetorical conventions that characterize communication in a particular discipline. The Participating Courses, then, are not special writing courses in the disciplines; they are simply courses taught by faculty who have attended the workshops offered by the Center for Teaching and who choose to make use of the principles and methods taught there.

8. Writing in the Professions is a sophomore/junior elective course that focuses on written communication problems in the professions, especially though not exclusively those associated with communicating with lay audiences. The course also has a research and development function: it is intended to provide a place for evaluating pedagogical innovations in writing-across-the-curriculum; for developing and evaluating teaching materials and techniques for use in faculty workshops, the Designated Writing Courses, and the Participating Courses; and in some cases, for carrying out research on problems having to do with language use in the university.

11

Teaching as an Act of Unknowing

Charles I. Schuster

Carl, a third-year teaching assistant, walks into his English 101 classroom. It is the fourth week of the term. In his briefcase, he has copies of two essays written by students in the class. One of them perfectly illustrates a point he has been trying to make for the past two weeks about voice and commitment. For all its virtues of correctness and clarity, the essay is wrapped in a shroud of grayness: the writer has concealed herself within the guise of academic neutrality. Carl's students, having gained just enough awareness of his own preferences and critical vocabulary, will (he knows) value the essay for its virtues and criticize it for its inability to give voice in ways that connect writers to readers. He anticipates the discussion, shaping it in his mind, imagining himself directing his students (like a conductor—with essay as score and freshmen as orchestra) toward an exhilarating crescendo. It is the music of the spheres that he hears as he crosses into the classroom.

But a note of dissonance creeps into his orchestral suite. Its source is the other essay that lies nestled tightly against its sister. This essay resists him. Having read it three times, he cannot quite figure out its voice, its intention, its conflictual treatment of its subject. Does the author know what she's doing? If so, then why does the focus shift so abruptly twice during the essay? How should he read the coarse language in the fourth paragraph? What about the mocking voice in the parenthetical passages? Is the subject being parodied? The author? Carl himself?

As his 101 writers form into groups to share and discuss the opening paragraphs of their current writing-in-progress, Carl must decide which essay to workshop at the end of class. There is no incorrect choice; both essays have much to teach the students. Only one of the essays, however, has much to teach Carl.

Susan's basic writing class is developing in fine fashion. The students are interacting productively, both as writers and as speakers. One of Susan's most successful strategies is to start nearly every class day by asking the students to write on a topic that Susan gives them. Recent examples include the relationship between grades and education, abortion rights for women under the age of eighteen, rock lyrics and censorship. Susan prints each topic on the board (or hands it out on ditto) and the students write for five to ten minutes; then she collects their responses, reads them quickly, and selects two or three of the best-written and most provocative to read aloud the following class day.

During midsemester, Susan schedules a "health checkup day" in which she devotes an entire session to a discussion of how the class is doing, what the students have accomplished so far, and which new goals and procedures would make for a most successful second half of the semester. During discussion, Frances, one of Susan's most confident students, makes a suggestion: "Why don't you let us create the in-class writing topics? We could then read them and choose the ones *we* like best."

"And you would have to write too—on topics that *we* think up," adds Peter. "We'd get to read *you!*"

Immediately some of the other students agree with Fran and Peter, while most simply sit there cautiously, waiting to see how Susan will respond. Having the students create the in-class writing assignments is risky business; Susan fears that Ed, for example, would ask everyone (including her) to write about their first sexual experience, while Maxine might require a short essay about a time when everyone in the class said or did something that was racist. Furthermore, Susan's role would change in part from teacher to student, from authorizer of writing to author. Susan's control of the class might begin to slip, her power erode. Some of the topics might produce "bad" writing, might frustrate and anger the students. They might choose poor examples to read aloud in the class. Yet there is something exciting and liberating in the prospect as well; the students might develop confidence in themselves as writers and readers by taking charge of their own daily writing assignments. They would have to learn how to negotiate topics and responses within their own class community. They might challenge each other to write in ways that she could not. Susan ruminates, all eyes focused to the front of the classroom, a space she will have to relinquish during "writing response" time if she follows Frances's suggestion. She is unsure what to do. Whatever she decides, the class dynamic will alter.

The two situations I have just described are familiar to me. They should be: both are versions of my own experiences and those of teaching assistants I have observed over the years. As these exempla imply, teaching is a negotiated space. Indeed, although some teachers don't think much about it, teaching is one of the most obvious ways in which we put theory into practice. It reveals our most basic educative principles, our most cherished notions about what it means to learn. What I want to offer in the follow pages is a particular kind of teaching which draws from the theories of Mikhail Bakhtin and puts into practice a kind of pedagogy I call "teaching as an act of unknowing."

Let me say first of all that the very phrase "teaching as an act of unknowing" seems like an oxymoron. How can teachers teach if they lack knowledge of their subject? Without "knowing," what enables teachers to teach? What would they say to their students? What would they do in the classroom? Doesn't this phrase authorize ignorance by suggesting that the less teachers know, the better off they are?

No. "Unknowing" is not ignorance; it is, rather, an attitude toward students and subjects, a philosophy of learning. It can't be faked, it is not a pedagogical trick, and it is not a strategy that works 100 percent of the time. To state these conditions is not to undermine what I am proposing: no effective teaching strategy can be faked or is a trick (like sawing someone in half) or works every time one steps into a classroom. After all, if teaching were open to prescription, all we'd need to do is memorize a set of methodologies and find our problems solved for life. The classroom is a negotiated space; much of what happens there depends upon shifting conditions, on the quicksilver nature of student-teacher interactions, on classroom context. Part of what makes an instructor effective—particularly one who teaches that most difficult of all subjects, composition—is the ability to respond to the endlessly variable problems and confusions posed by each subject and classroom full of students. I don't much believe in sentence combining, for example, but I have taught it (at times, as my exclusive focus) and used it to illustrate what is more important to me: how to create style and voice for oneself as a writer. I don't believe in teaching grammar as a method of teaching writing, but I have taught grammar both as a knowledge base for gaining the confidence to critique the essay and as a deconstructive subject that has more to say about what we don't know than what we do concerning written English. I am not at all sure that I have inevitably succeeded with these subjects, but what they have taught me is the importance of being able to shift one's ground within the classroom without sacrificing principles and essential values. In some of those classrooms, I taught my subject in the role of expert, as someone who has specific knowledge and insight to offer students; in others, I constructed my role differently, as someone engaged in thinking through a subject alongside my students.

Teaching as an act of unknowing describes this latter form of pedagogy, one in which teachers engage dialogically with students in the complicated and continuous working out of problems in and through spoken and written conversations. The key terms here are "conversation" and "dialogically" because many teachers of English would probably conceive of themselves as necessarily filling the classroom with teacher talk and student response as part of their training and responsibility. What I am arguing for is a repositioning in the politics of the classroom, a movement away from the current-traditional paradigm which privileges teacher talk over student talk, which operates within a stipulatory understanding of the classroom as a place where teachers speak and listen from a position of assumed knowledge while students speak and listen from a position of implied ignorance. That teachers possess more power than students within the classroom is undeniable: teachers create the curriculum, give assignments, dispense grades. What is not undeniable is that instructors must inevitably position themselves as powerful, pseudo-omniscient Superteachers in relation to their students, who then become hapless and helpless spectators.

Most of us teach as we were taught, and unfortunately that often means we enact the current-traditional paradigm in our classrooms. Let me offer an example. A few weeks ago I observed a first-semester teaching assistant. Earnest and serious about teaching, Flavio (as I'll call him) wanted to teach his students about the structure of an essay, in this instance "The Case of Harry Houdini" by Daniel Mark Epstein. His method of achieving this goal was to write an outline of the essay's structure on the blackboard, soliciting suggestions as he went along from the students as to the ways Epstein organized his information. The students volunteered ideas and suggestions; the instructor wrote them on the board; the outline veered out of shape, with both instructor and students increasingly confused as to the putative relation between outline and essay. When I spoke with Flavio afterward, he freely confessed that the outline was ultimately as confusing to him as it was to the students and me, but he was trapped into continuing as if he knew what he were doing and proceeded thus until the end of the hour. Why? Because he was the teacher, teachers possess superior knowledge, and his job was to teach what he knows—even if that job becomes impossible because either his knowledge or his instructional method is insufficient. Even were Flavio a more experienced instructor, able to use class responses to fulfill his Platonic model, the methodology would be the same: teacher defining class interaction, forcing students into narrow, pre-conceived roles. It is as if students are scripted subjects, characters in a play, their dialogue written out ahead of time by the instructor.

After the class, Flavio himself suggested some alternatives. He could have solicited outlines from the students. He could have had them outline the opening section of the essay individually and then called upon students to write their attempts on the board. Such moves, I think, would have helped. But his teaching at this early stage of his career is open to more radical critique. That is, he could have asked his students questions about the essay's structure and development *to which he did not have the answers*. For example, he could have asked why the essay opens with an account of the grandfa-ther's recollection of Houdini, or why the essay begins with the historical and factual but ends with the mysterious and inexplicable. Moreover, he could have asked students to pursue these questions within a small-group setting or in a debate format which excludes the instructor as participant or center of authority. He might have decided that a consideration of structure might need to be subordi-nated within a discussion of other topics—Epstein's intentions, pre-sumed audience, rhetorical strategies—and that these issues were best raised by means of a series of writing/talking/large-group/small-group activities which Flavio could initiate but not dictate, based on ques-tions that Flavio might ask but could not answer. That is, Flavio might place "The Case of Harry Houdini" within an interrogatory mode that leaves both the text and the variety of readings it provokes open to interpretation and debate. Such an approach would necessar-ily engage teacher and students in conversation, as opposed to lecture or question/answer response. It would offer a conception of class-room space as open, as a place where talk ranges freely and possesses qualities of ambivalence, confusion, negotiation, free give-and-take. Such classrooms are both more exciting *and* more dangerous, for within their most contested borders authority becomes less a line than a trace. When teaching is an act of unknowing, the classroom becomes transformed into a threshold space, a destabilized arena of ideas which offers the possibility of a genuine engagement of individuals with each other and with the subject of the course.

This concept of "the threshold" is one I have drawn from the work of Mikhail Bakhtin. In *Problems of Dostoyevsky's Poetics,* Bakhtin in part accounts for Dostoyevsky's genius by describing him as a threshold author, someone who positions himself and his characters on physical and metaphysical borders. These marginalized spaces are both aspects of the plot and metaphors for Dostoyevsky's artistic point of view. In his discussion of *Crime and Punishment,* for example, Bakhtin writes that Raskolnikov

> lives, in essence, on a threshold: his narrow room, a "coffin" . . . opens directly onto the *landing of the staircase,* and he never locks his door, even when he goes out. . . . The threshold, the foyer, the corridor, the landing, the stairway, its steps, doors opening onto the stairway, gates to front and back yards, and beyond these, the city: squares, streets, facades, taverns, dens, bridges, gutters. This is the space of the novel. And in fact absolutely nothing here ever loses touch with the threshold, there is no interior of drawing rooms, dining rooms, halls, stu-dios, bedrooms where biographical life unfolds and where events take place in the novels of writers such as Turgenev, Tolstoy, and Goncharov. (*Problems* 170)

According to Bakhtin, Dostoyevsky situates his characters quite liter-ally within contested spaces, ambiguous territories that represent shifting boundaries. To be fully inside a room or outside in an open field is to place oneself in a defined territory; to walk on the edge of a forest is to negotiate a terrain that exists as a conflictual, ambiguous site. If we apply Bakhtin's concept to the school environment, we see that a classroom is (often) a well-defined space; in it, an instructor is considered to be in charge and students are to do as they are told. Contrastingly, a doorway, a hallway, a set of steps upon which stu-dents move up and down—these are more contested areas in which identities and authorities become confused. In such spaces, inversions can occur: teachers and students can change places, mock each other, assume masks of innocence and betrayal. Threshold spaces undermine conventional and accepted ways of thinking and acting; they destabilize life, making it ambiguous; they maintain the potential of eroding the earth beneath one's feet. Life on the threshold is disorienting. Part of my intention is to move this concept of contested space into the classroom so as to complicate the unfolding events that occur there.

Bakhtin extends this concept of the threshold, ultimately arguing for a kind of threshold mythos in Dostoyevsky. A case in point, according to Bakhtin, is Dostoyevsky's fascination with the world of gamblers:

> People from various (hierarchical) positions in life, once crowded around the roulette table, are made equal by the rules of the game and in the face of fortune, chance. Their behavior at the roulette table in no way corresponds to the role they play in ordinary life. The atmosphere of gambling is an atmosphere of sudden and quick changes of fate, of instantaneous rises and falls, that is, of crownings/decrownings. The *stake* is similar to a *crisis;* a person feels himself *on the threshold.* And the time of gambling is a special time: here, too, a minute is equal to years. (*Problems* 171)

In his analysis of the trope of gambling in Dostoyevskian novels, Bakhtin describes a number of stipulatory features which characterize its threshold status and which are significant as well in our discussion of the classroom. For one thing, gambling is a game, a field of play with artificial but essential rules of conduct and fair play. As such, the activity is both intensely real and yet artificial; it matters intensely but only within its own domain. As I have written elsewhere ("Situational Sequencing" and "The Power of Play"), this notion of game and play is central to the writing classroom, which must become simultaneously a place where writing matters intensely but also where students can be creative, experimental risk takers.

Gambling—like other threshold experiences—equalizes the various players: rich and poor, aristocrat and peasant surround the roulette wheel on equal terms. Talk flows freely, if intensely. The fortunes of the various players rise and fall with rapidity; a sense of crisis permeates the atmosphere. Participants strive to control their own future, although they often submit to a sense of fate and fortune which all but overwhelms them. For Bakhtin, one of the central features of gambling, penal servitude, traveling through alien territories, and other forms of threshold experience is their quality of being *"'life taken out of life'* (that is, taken out of common ordinary life)" (*Problems* 172). Threshold experiences are dramatic, even melodramatic, and they occur in a different kind of time; in some sense they seem virtually timeless, not bound by our usual understanding of beginning, middle, and end.

I don't want to exaggerate the importance of the threshold in relation to teaching, particularly teaching writing. I am not, for example, advocating that the classroom become a gambling hall or that students' fates be determined by a throw of the die. What I am advocating is that all of us as instructors position ourselves—at least at times—within a threshold ideology of teaching, one in which traditional views and positions are inverted, play becomes a dominant field of action, students and teachers engage in a genuine conversation in which all participants possess equivalent claims as speakers and listeners. In such classrooms, traditional hierarchies (teacher over student, "smart" student over "dumb" student) disappear. Students debate openly and with intensity as their fates and fortunes shift continuously because they begin to see that ideas, issues, and oral and written responses are not simply "right" or "wrong," but rather both and neither. In the process, students play out different roles for themselves in conversation and writing; they work through a variety of perspectives. As John Trimbur has stated, "To learn is to change: learning implies a shift in social standing—a transition from one status and identity to another and a reorientation of social allegiances" ("Collaborative Learning" 90). Such a view is the very essence of threshold—and of teaching as an act of unknowing.

Bakhtin's concept of the "threshold" is a particularized aspect of that genre which Bakhtin calls "novel," another concept which possesses considerable implications for teachers of writing and literature. It is not possible to describe fully what Bakhtin means by this genre, but it is clear that his view of "novel" is not limited to fictions of 150 pages or more. Instead, he sees novel as a kind of antigenre, not a formal category but a qualitative one. Novelistic texts (in the Bakhtinian sense) are "dialogical." They are open-ended, experimental, discursive, loosely shaped. They are situated in the present and celebrate the impossibility of finalizing people, events, utterances. In *The Dialogical Imagination,* Bakhtin offers many descriptive phrases to describe "novel." In the novel, "a speaking and conversing man [i.e., individual] is the central image" (24). The novel "speculates in what is unknown" (32). It is "a developing genre" (33). The novel is constructed "on concrete social speech diversity" (412), that is, it is situated in the midst of a variety of speakers who speak in a great variety of tones, accents, and styles. The author in these dialogical narratives functions less as a controlling and determining force than as one of many speakers in a multiple dialogue: "The author participates in the novel (he is omnipresent in it) with *almost no direct language of his own*. The language of the novel is a *system* of languages that mutually and ideologically interanimate each other" (47). In essence, the author's speech in a novel is charged by and refracted through the speech of the characters whose tones, nuances, and attitudes infiltrate it. Direct authorial speech about a character or event tends to be replaced by irony, parody, indirect quotation, multiaccented discourses, laughter. The author in a dialogical narrative does not reserve for her/himself the final word. Quite the contrary, "the author's discourse about a character is organized as discourse about *someone actually present,* someone who hears him (the author) and is *capable of answering him*" (*Problems* 63). Thus, one of the qualities that characterize novelistic forms is that they possess a multiplicity of speakers and voices, a quality that Bakhtin at one point describes as "polyphonic" (in *Problems*). In a way, then, a novel (in Bakhtinian terms) becomes the creation of both its author and its characters, rather than a construct of the author alone.

This multiple creation occurs in part because of the way Bakhtin repositions the rhetorical triangle. For Bakhtin, speaker, subject, and listener are equivalent forces within an utterance (see Voloshinov). Bakhtin renames "subject" as "hero," and the hero of a text can be anything from a character to a subject or an ideological position. The hero of *Great Expectations* is Pip; the hero of an essay on fate is fate; the hero of a state task-force report on basic competency in English is that complex of compositional abilities that enables a student to be a college writer. From the Bakhtinian point of view, listeners and heroes enter into a discourse as full participants along with the speaker and have speaking voices: that is, they also shape and influence language. Bakhtin writes: "For the author the hero is not 'he' and not 'I' but a fully valid 'thou,' that is, another and other autonomous 'I' ('thou art')" (*Problems* 63). The listener, too, plays a central role in discourse: indeed, every utterance is directed toward a listener who shapes the very theme and texture of that utterance. Moreover, every listener is herself both a real and a potential speaker. Discourse is a complex double helix in which every participant is a speaker/listener engaged with a hero. To enact a dialogical pedagogy in the classroom is to author a class as novel. Indeed, it is useful to think of the classroom not in terms of personalities or responsibilities, but rather as a text which is authored. After all, like a novel, the classroom has characters and a plot. It progresses temporally: things happen, characters appear and disappear, successes follow failures, people listen and speak. Like novels, classes have settings, contexts, conflicts, resolutions, climaxes, and denouements. If we agree that a class can be understood as a narrative text in this sense, then who writes it? Clearly the instructor has that responsibility, but from a Bakhtinian perspective, so do our students, who function as speaking subjects.

Such a revisionary view of teaching is in some ways made easier by the fact that in a classroom setting, students are both heroes *and* listeners, although the subject of "English" is also a hero that enters into the novelistic text. In a composition class, for example, I might begin by having all of us introduce ourselves in some extensive way to begin the process of coming to perceive ourselves as equivalent "thou arts." From there we might begin a series of reading/writing assignment sequences that are provisional, open-ended, reflexive. That is, I might ask students to consider the subject of art and culture. We might read essays by Susan Sontag, John Berger, E. H. Gombrich, John Ruskin, Alice Walker. We might view a film, debate its merits, and write a review; listen to a lecture by a media specialist, take continuous notes while watching six hours of television, and from them develop an anthropological perspective concerning popular culture; create collages and critique them as popular art. In creating such a curriculum, I am indeed authoring a class, developing a structure and fulfilling my contractual responsibilities. My role within this curriculum, however, is not that of expert; quite the contrary, I know less about most of the subjects we write about than do many of my students. What I do know something about (at least one hopes so) is how to teach, how to move students forward as writers and thinkers. Thus, my role is to engage in acts of discovery along with my students, to foster dialogue and debate, to foster individual and collaborative structures within which learning will occur.

Such a dialogical classroom is not controllable. It does not fit within a neat and orderly description; its twists and turns hardly accommodate a detailed syllabus distributed during the first week of class. Part of what makes such a class succeed is the degree to which I, as teacher, adjust and revise the class in response to student interests, needs, actions, and reactions. Like the dialogical novel, the dialogical classroom is created as a result of the relation among author, character, listener. It unfolds, often unexpectedly, as participants commit themselves to surprising intellectual pursuits. To accomplish these aims, instructors must teach as unknowers by placing themselves— and their students—in unfamiliar settings, speculative frames of mind. They must live on the borders of their knowledge, those edges where ideas interpenetrate, like the cellular exchanges that take place through osmosis. Bakhtin puts it this way:

> Human thought becomes genuine thought, that is, an idea, only under conditions of living contact with another and alien thought, a thought embodied in someone else's voice, that is, in someone else's consciousness expressed in discourse. At that point of contact between voice-consciousnesses the idea is born and lives. (*Problems* 88)

For such "living contact" to occur, students must be alive to their own ideas, their own experience, their own ability as intellectuals. Walker Percy calls this state of mind "sovereignty," and it enables students to engage in discovery in relation to their academic subject (46–63).

An essential feature of this pedagogy is the nature of question and response. If it is to be dialogical, question and response must mutually engage all participants. It most characteristically takes the form of Socratic dialogue, a genre which Bakhtin considers constitutive of the novel. For Bakhtin, Socratic dialogues (of which only those by Plato and Xenophon are extant) represent a "dialogic means of seeking truth [which] is counterposed to *official* monologism, which pretends to *possess a ready-made truth,* and it is counterposed to the naive self-confidence of those people who think that they know something, that is, who think that they possess certain truths" (*Problems* 110). The means by which Socratic dialogue is created are *syncrisis* and *anacrisis*. Syncrisis "is the juxtaposition of various points of view on a specific object"; anacrisis is "a means for eliciting and provoking the words of one's interlocutor, forcing him to express his opinion and express it thoroughly" (*Problems* 110). To foster Socratic dialogue, therefore, teachers must structure class so that a variety of opinions, ideas, viewpoints, and arguments come to bear on a single topic, a single essay or idea. And they must discover means to provoke response, not through threat or forms of evaluative torture, but rather by being constructive, by creating a class of sympathetic listeners, by being outrageous—any of a variety of means by which students become willing to engage with a subject through talk and writing.

In a classroom that privileges such dialogue, teacher and students must situate themselves and their intellectual concerns within threshold subjects, must enlarge their intellectual capacity to engage threshold oppositions. When I ask students (1) to write an editorial denouncing drug abuse, (2) to compose three journal entries from a crack addict, and (3) to assume the roles of crack dealer, police officer, mayor, and inner-city politician in a roundtable discussion focusing on the root causes of drug abuse, I am encouraging them to complicate their thinking and understand oppositional values and concepts. When I ask students to read dramatically divergent essays on racism and affirmative action, and then to write a series of exploratory essays analyzing and exploring the assumptions and consequences of the various viewpoints, I am encouraging them to balance themselves intellectually on a threshold. When students discuss topics and essays independently in small groups, oppositional points of view occur inevitably. When students meet together in collaborative writing groups to critique and discuss their own essays, dialogic interaction becomes possible and students participate in that simultaneously exhilarating and frightening experience: authoring themselves as they author their own work. Whatever the strategy, students need to become sovereign intellects who can work with teachers, not under them. They need as well to develop that most useful category of critical thinking: the capacity to explore and sustain ambiguity and ambivalence, to consider conflictual attitudes and ideas so that they can be thought through and evaluated. Maxine Hong Kingston states this same objective poetically when she describes her training as a woman warrior: "I learned to make my mind large, as the universe is large, so that there is room for paradoxes" (35). To teach as an act of unknowing inevitably depends on paradox because questions posed by teachers have no single or correct answer, and classroom activities engage students as interactive, unpredictable, equivalent speaking subjects.

If teaching a class can be compared to creating a Bakhtinian novel, one might well ask who is the ultimate reader of that text? In many situations the answer is daunting: the chair of the department, who is evaluating teacher performance; the parents, who are paying for it; the tenure-review committee; the curriculum supervisor; the dean.

These "readers" may well misperceive the free flow of the dialogical classroom as chaos or confusion; they may prefer the orderly top-down flow of information that is typical of most classrooms. Ultimately, however, the most significant readers of this text are the very individuals who write it—the teacher and students who spend a semester learning how to learn. Although there is undoubtedly value in lecture, demonstration, and other forms of current-traditional teaching (which must always be used in conjunction with the kind of approach I am advocating), my preference for teaching as an act of unknowing rests on my belief that the meaning of such a classroom continually shifts; it has an interactive dynamic that frustrates rigid analysis and monologic descriptions. In my experience at least, dialogical forms of pedagogy are more likely to make a real difference to students, to become internalized, because they force students to become engaged, to act and perform and *learn* rather than simply to memorize and repeat.

Teaching as an act of unknowing is an outgrowth of Bakhtinian theory; as such, it derives its theoretical rationale from concepts of the threshold, novel, and dialogism. To teach in this way requires a philosophic/conceptual reordering of the relations between teacher and student, teacher and subject, teacher and school—that is, a radical restructuring of our educational values. One of the aspects that makes it so difficult to achieve is that it depends not upon external factors— the room, textbooks, teaching strategies—but upon an internalized reconception of speaking and listening, readers and writers. The two examples with which I opened this essay are cases in point: Carl and Susan can teach what they know—or they can teach as an act of unknowing, one which involves them as learners as much as teachers. Clearly my preference is that teachers and students engage in the problems of a class collaboratively, in a shared spirit of discovery and inquiry. Teaching in this way depends on a kind of "unknowing," but ultimately what is learned far exceeds what is taught.

12

*H*e Takes the Teaching of Writing Seriously: A Bibliography of Works by William F. Irmscher

Richard Tracey

For over four decades, William F. Irmscher has played a large part in determining what it means to study rhetoric and composition. He directed freshman composition programs for over a quarter of a century and directed a teacher training program almost that long, edited *College Composition and Communication* and chaired the Conference on College Composition and Communication, and presided over the National Council of Teachers of English. Professor Irmscher's career is marked both by his emphasis on the quality of composition instruction as applied rhetoric and by his steady advocacy of increased professionalism at all levels of rhetoric/composition teaching, kindergarten through college. For over forty years, he has prodded us to become better rhetoric/composition teachers by urging us to consider the Burkean dramatism—the agent, purpose, scene, act, and means—in our teaching. It is not just coincidental, then, that his career almost exactly parallels the emergence of rhetoric/composition as a respected academic discipline. As the following biography and bibliography testify, there is a cause-effect relationship between Professor Irmscher's career and the academic discipline that others now inherit from him.

William F. Irmscher was born 11 April 1920 in Louisville, Kentucky, where he spent his first twenty-two years. He attended the Louisville Public Schools, from which he graduated in January 1937. His father had died the year earlier and money was scarce, so Irmscher entered Clark College of Commerce, completing a four-month course in typing, shorthand, bookkeeping, and "quick math" (calculating rapidly in one's head) so that he could find work. He soon took a job as a bank teller, but his sister Esther insisted that her brother should attend college, offering to pay his way from her earnings. So the next fall Irmscher entered the University of Louisville, from which he earned his Bachelor of Arts degree in 1941, in English and history.

That same year, Irmscher began his teaching career, as a junior high school English instructor. World War II, however, interrupted his career at the end of that first year, when, in June 1942, Irmscher was inducted into the United States Army. He served as an enlisted man in the infantry from 1942 through 1945, serving overseas in 1944 and 1945 in England, France, Belgium, and Germany, and finally with the occupation forces in Czechoslovakia.

Returning home from his wartime service, Irmscher took advantage of the GI Bill to earn his master's and doctoral degrees in English. First he enrolled at the University of Chicago, where, in 1947, he earned his M.A. in English literature in four quarters. The next fall he enrolled in the English doctoral program at Indiana University, studying Renaissance literature and minoring in English language study. There, as a teaching assistant, he began the four-decade career in college composition that continued through 1988. He earned his Ph.D. from Indiana in 1950, with a dissertation on John Donne's love poetry.

That year, Professor Irmscher joined the English Department of the University of Arizona, where he taught Renaissance literature, the drama, and freshman composition. In 1954, he was appointed Director of Freshman English at Arizona. In 1960, Professor Irmscher left Tucson for Seattle, succeeding Glenn Leggett as Director of Freshman Composition at the University of Washington. He continued in that post until 1983, having served as director at Washington for twenty-three years. In fact, adding to this his six years directing the freshman program at Arizona makes a total of twenty-nine years directing university freshman English programs, which must represent some sort of record for longevity in that capacity.

At Washington, Professor Irmscher established and supervised the Masters of Arts for Teachers (MAT) in English and directed numerous doctoral dissertations in rhetoric/composition, including those of five of the contributors to this volume (Anderson, Buley-Meissner, Chappell, Farris, and Tracey). He also conducted a Summer Seminar for College Teachers for the National Endowment for the Humanities and directed secondary English teachers' institutes funded by the National Defense Education Act, as well as one institute for the College Entrance Examination Board that was funded as a trial to prove to the government that English was worthy of federal support. Irmscher's growing national reputation led, in 1972, to a long-running relationship with Holt, Rinehart and Winston, for whom he wrote ten textbooks—six for the college market and four for the secondary school market—plus his essential reference book for writing teachers at all levels, *Teaching Expository Writing* (1979). It was in the first edition of his *Holt Guide to English* (1972) that Professor Irmscher introduced Kenneth Burke's dramatistic pentad as a heuristic for teaching and learning expository writing. This heuristic pentad was quickly embraced by the rhetoric/composition community and is now a staple of prewriting instruction.

Certainly, Kenneth Burke has been the presiding theoretical presence in Professor Irmscher's work. Irmscher's interpretation of Burke's pentad serves as the organizing principle of both *Teaching Expository Writing* and the syllabus of the freshman composition course Professor Irmscher directed at the University of Washington. Also, his work on what, in *The Holt Guide,* he terms "the syntax of thought" knowingly reflects Burke's famous definition of literary form as the arousing and fulfillment of desires. And his desire that we acknowledge intuition echoes Burke's preference for intellectual analyses of language, not the scientism of experimental treatments in composition research. But Professor Irmscher, like Kenneth Burke, is more than the sum of his publications. Although Burke took him to task at the 1977 MLA Convention for using the dramatistic pentad as a practical tool to explore human experience, and not just as a theoretical tool to explore symbolic texts, Burke did acknowledge that both applications of the pentad have their own relevance (see Irmscher's "Kenneth Burke"). Professor Irmscher, too, is an inclusive thinker, embracing both theory and practice, to the exclusion of neither. In Irmscher, as in Burke, it's all one: theory and practice are different ways of thinking about each other.

This Burkean synthesis of both theory and practice is seen as much in Professor Irmscher's teaching as in his scholarship. Whether teaching freshmen composition or directing dissertations, he is an inclusive mentor, allowing students to forge their own paths, not just follow his own. His usual technique is for students to experience ideas concretely—that is, through direct practice, usually involving writing as thinking/learning. Then, by reflecting theoretically on this practical experience, students move from practice to theory, as Burke moves from anecdote to philosophy. In this oblique learning style, Professor Irmscher's students may—to paraphrase Burke—borrow from others, develop from others, use one text to comment dialectically upon another, theorize, engage in practical discourse, and review these discursions to theorize again.

Concurrent with his duties at the University of Washington, Professor Irmscher served the National Council of Teachers of English in various important capacities, up to and including NCTE President, 1982–83. But it is in his service to the NCTE's Conference on College Composition and Communication that Professor Irmscher has had the greatest impact on our profession. His relationship with the CCCC dates back to 1959, when he attended his first CCCC meeting. Twenty years later, in 1979, he served as chair of the CCCC. And in total, he served thirteen years on the CCCC Executive Committee. From 1965 through 1974, he was editor of *College Composition and Communication,* building it into the preeminent journal in the field of college rhetoric/composition. As *CCC* editor, Professor Irmscher helped establish rhetoric/composition as a significant area of academic research with a swelling base of scholarship. He published the first or seminal articles by such people as Alton Becker, Ann Berthoff, Francis Christensen, Frank D'Angelo, Richard Gebhardt, James Kinneavy, Richard Larson, Janice Lauer, Lee Odell, Mina Shaughnessy, and Ross Winterowd. Some of these scholars' *CCC* articles were reedited by Professor Irmscher in *The Sentence and the Paragraph* (1967), one of the longest-lived NCTE titles ever published.

Professor Irmscher has also served on the editorial advisory board for other journals in our field: *Teaching English in the Two-Year College* (1978–80), *College English* (1985–present), and *Writing on the Edge* (1988–present). His experience as *CCC* editor prompted him in 1978 to propose to the CCCC Executive Committee that they publish a series of monographs in college rhetoric/composition studies—pieces too long for *CCC* but too short for a typical NCTE-published book. The committee supported Professor Irmscher's proposal, which took shape in 1984 as the Studies in Writing and Rhetoric series, published for CCCC by Southern Illinois University Press.

When the third edition of his *Holt Guide to English* was selected as the basis for the telecourse *The Write Course* (1985), Professor Irmscher signed on as a consultant to this Annenberg Foundation–funded series for freshman composition. An alternate third edition of *The Holt Guide* (1985) remains the adopted text for colleges that offer credit for this telecourse. It was also in 1985 that Professor Irmscher retired from the University of Washington, although he continued to teach as an emeritus professor until the end of 1988.

This brief summary of Professor Irmscher's curriculum vitae is rounded out by the bibliography that follows. It is the bibliography of one who, for over four decades, has helped shape what it means to study rhetoric/composition by probing thoughtfully into writing instruction. "I take the teaching of writing seriously," he writes at the beginning of *Teaching Expository Writing*. He embraces both rhetorical theory and applied rhetoric—that is, composition—as the two poles of a continuum, such that writing instruction is a different way of thinking about rhetoric. To know this is to understand that taking writing seriously is not to engage in a lowly pedantic enterprise but to concern oneself with the highest study of all human relations.

Indeed, Professor Irmscher's longevity in the capacity of composition director encompasses the unique moment that he grasped in the history of our discipline. He became a composition director at a time when directing a composition program was either a career stepping-stone or else a dead-end job. He stepped down from being a composition director at a time when directing such a program, at least within the rhetoric/composition community that he helped create, had become a respectable career.

The various entries of Professor Irmscher's bibliography urge us to think dramatistically about our teaching of rhetoric/composition by joining him in taking the teaching of writing seriously.

Books

"The Conventional Aspects of John Donne as a Love Poet." Diss. Indiana U, 1950.
Ways of Writing. New York: McGraw, 1969.
The Holt Guide to English: A Contemporary Handbook of Rhetoric, Language and Literature. New York: Holt, 1972.
What Do You Do to Teach Composition? [Instructor's manual for *The*

Holt Guide to English: A Contemporary Handbook of Rhetoric, Language and Literature, 1st ed.] New York: Holt, 1972.

The Nature of Literature: Writing on Literary Topics. New York: Holt, 1975.

The Holt Guide to English: A Contemporary Handbook of Rhetoric, Language and Literature. 2d ed. New York: Holt, 1976.

What Do You Do to Teach Composition? 2d ed. [Instructors manual for *The Holt Guide to English: A Contemporary Handbook of Rhetoric, Language and Literature,* 2d ed.] New York: Holt, 1976.

Teaching Expository Writing. New York: Holt, 1979.

The Holt Guide to English: A Comprehensive Handbook of Rhetoric, Language and Literature. 3d ed. New York: Holt, 1981.

Instructors Manual for The Holt Guide to English: A Comprehensive Handbook of Rhetoric, Language and Literature: *3rd ed.* New York: Holt, [1981].

With James P. Hall et al. *Holt English: Language and Writing.* Grade 9. New York: Holt, 1983.

With James P. Hall et al. *Holt English: Language and Writing.* Grade 10. New York: Holt, 1983.

With James P. Hall et al. *Holt English: Language and Writing.* Grade 11. New York: Holt, 1983.

With James P. Hall et al. *Holt English: Language and Writing.* Grade 12. New York: Holt, 1983.

Teachers Guide for Holt English: Language and Writing: *Grade 12.* New York: Holt, 1983.

With Harryette Stover. *The Holt Guide to English.* Alternate 3d ed. New York: Holt, 1985.

Books Edited

With E. R. Hagemann. *The Language of Ideas.* Indianapolis: Bobbs, 1963.

Man and Warfare: Thematic Readings for Composition. Boston: Little, 1964.

The Sentence and the Paragraph. Champaign, IL: NCTE, 1967.

Contributions to Books

"The Freshman Composition Program at the University of Washington." *Freshman Composition.* Ed. Jasper P. Neel. Options for the Teaching of Eng. 2. New York: MLA, 1978. 63–69.

"William Irmscher's Assignment." *What Makes Writing Good.* Ed. William E. Coles, Jr., and James Vopat. Lexington, MA: Heath, 1985. 17–20.

"Kenneth Burke." *Traditions of Inquiry.* Ed. John Brereton. New York: Oxford UP, 1985. 103–35.

"TA Training: A Period of Discovery." *Training the New Teacher of College Composition.* Ed. Charles W. Bridges. Urbana, IL: NCTE, 1986. 27–36.

Contributions to Reference Books

"Case"; "Clause"; "Comparison"; "Conjugation"; "Declension"; "Gender"; "Infinitive"; "Interjection"; "Mood"; "Parsing"; "Parts of Speech"; "Person"; "Phonics"; "Preposition"; "Syntax"; "Voice." *World Book Encyclopedia.* 1974–90 eds.

"Adjective"; "Adverb"; "Antecedent"; "Apposition"; "Article"; "Gerund"; "Grammar"; "Noun"; "Number"; "Participle"; "Pronoun"; "Sentence"; "Tense"; "Verb." *World Book Encyclopedia.* 1975–90 eds.

"Basic English." *World Book Encyclopedia.* 1976–90 eds.

"Abbreviation"; "Index." *World Book Encyclopedia.* 1983–90 eds.

"Antonym"; "Heteronym"; "Homonym." *World Book Encyclopedia.* 1988–90 eds.

Journal Edited

College Composition and Communication 16–24 (1965–73).

Journal Articles

"U. of Arizona Revises Freshman English Program." *Arizona English Bulletin* 1 (1959): 19–20.

"University of Arizona." *Arizona English Bulletin* 1 (1959): 25–26.

"The English Institute: Notes on Progress." *Arizona English Bulletin* 5 (1962): 27–28.

"One Down, Number Two to Go." *The College of Education Record* [U of Washington] 29 (1963): 39–42.

"An Apology for Literature." *English Journal* 52 (1963): 252+. Rpt. in condensed form in *Reading in High School* 1 (1963): 25–26.

"The Four Freedoms of the Student Writer." *Oregon Council Newsletter* [Oregon Council of Teachers of English] Spring 1968: 4+.

"Reflections of an Editor." *Freshman English News* 2.1 (1973): 4+.

"Analogy as an Approach to Rhetorical Theory." *College Composition and Communication* 27 (1976): 350–54.

"The Teaching of Writing in Terms of Growth." *English Journal* 66 (1977): 33–36.

"A Major Achievement." *English in the Two-Year College* 11 (1978): 2–3.

"Writing as a Way of Learning and Developing." *College Composition and Communication* 30 (1979): 240–44.

"Excellence Not an Elitist Concept: All Can Strive for It." *Focus: Teaching English Language Arts* [New Jersey Council of Teachers of English] 9 (Fall 1982): 44–45.

"Things That Get in the Way." *Washington English Journal* 5.2 (1983): 26–31.

"Toward Excellence." *The Illinois English Bulletin* 71.3 (1984): 10–17.

"Finding a Comfortable Identity." *College Composition and Communication* 38 (1987): 81–87.

Reviews

Rev. of *The Poetry of John Donne: A Study in Explication*, by Doniphan Louthan, and *Prayers: Selected and Edited from the Earliest Sources, with an Essay on Donne's Idea of Prayer*, ed. Herbert H. Umbach. *Arizona Quarterly* 7 (1951): 377–79.

Rev. of *The Seventeenth Century Background: Studies in the Thought of the Age in Relation to Poetry and Religion*, by Basil Wiley. *Arizona Quarterly* 10 (1954): 177.

Rev. of *Images and Themes in Five Poems by Milton*, by Rosemond Tuve. *Arizona Quarterly* 14 (1958): 79–81.

Rev. of *Milton*, by David Daiches. *Arizona Quarterly* 14 (1958): 178–80.

Rev. of *A New View of Congreve's* Way of the World, by Paul Mueschke and Miriam Mueschke. *Arizona Quarterly* 15 (1959): 86–87.

Rev. of *A Second Jacobean Journal: Being a Record of Those Things Most*

Talked of During the Years 1607 to 1610, by G. B. Harrison. *Arizona Quarterly* 15 (1959): 171–73.

Rev. of *In Praise of Love: An Introduction to the Love-Poetry of the Renaissance,* by Maurice Valency. *Arizona Quarterly* 15 (1959): 286–88.

Rev. of *The Short Story,* by Sean O'Faolain. *Studies in Short Fiction* 2 (1965): 298–99.

Rev. of *The Columbia-Viking Desk Encyclopedia,* ed. William Bridgwater et al. *College Composition and Communication* 18 (1967): 60.

Rev. of *Contemporary Authors. College Composition and Communication* 18 (1967): 60.

Rev. of *The New Wildhagen German Dictionary,* comp. Karl Wildhagen and Will Heracourt. *College Composition and Communication* 18 (1967): 59.

Rev. of *The Original Roget's Thesaurus of English Words and Phrases,* comp. Robert A. Dutch. *College Composition and Communication* 18 (1967): 60.

Rev. of *Rhetoric Faculty Handbook,* by the Rhetoric Program, U of Iowa. *College Composition and Communication* 18 (1967): 60.

Rev. of *House of All Nations,* by Christina Stead. *Wall Street Review of Books* 1 (1973): 234–36.

Rev. of *The Image of Australia: British Perception of the Australian Economy from the Eighteenth to the Twentieth Century,* by Craufurd D. W. Goodwin. *Wall Street Review of Books* 2 (1974): 90–92.

Rev. of *Teaching Composition: Ten Bibliographical Essays,* ed. Gary Tate. *College Composition and Communication* 28 (1977): 327–30.

Rev. of *Constructing Texts: Elements of a Theory of Composition and Style,* by George L. Dillon. *ADE Bulletin* 73 (1982): 58–59.

Rev. of *The Writer's Mind,* ed. Janice N. Hays et al. *College Composition and Communication* 35 (1984): 368–69.

Rev. of *The Making of Knowledge in Composition: Portrait of an Emerging Field,* by Stephen M. North. *Harvard Educational Review* 58 (1988): 513–16.

Information Services

"Quality for All." Presidential address. NCTE Convention. Denver, 18 Nov. 1983. ERIC ED 248 519.

"Acknowledging Intuition." Conference on College Composition and Communication. Kansas City, MO, 1 Apr. 1977. ERIC ED 150 640.

Miscellanea

"Freshman English Basic to University Studies." *After Hours* [U of Washington] 3.4 (1960): 2. Rpt. in *University of Washington Memo to Schools* Feb. 1961: 2.

"A Page for Macrorie." *College Composition and Communication* 16 (1965): 2.

"A Page for Squire." *College Composition and Communication* 18 (1967): 213.

"In Memoriam: Rev. Dr. Martin Luther King, Jr.: 1929–1968." *College Composition and Communication* 19 (1968): 105. Rpt. in *University of Illinois Speech and Theatre Alumni News* May 1968: 19.

"Alchemical Reflections." *AAP Newsletter* [Association of American Publishers] Nov. 1973: ii.

"Change of Editorship." *College Composition and Communication* 24 (1973): 365.

Foreword. *Composition and Its Teaching: Articles from* College Composition and Communication *During the Editorship of Edward P. J. Corbett.* Ed. Richard C. Gebhardt. Findlay: Ohio Council of Teachers of English Language Arts, 1979. 4–5.

"Inaugural Remarks: Meditations on a Professional Organization." Presidential address. NCTE Convention. Washington, 21 Nov. 1982. Excerpted by Jane Christensen and Diane Allen. *College English* 45 (1983): 53–56; *English Journal* 72.1 (1983): 90–91; *Language Arts* 60 (1983): 137–40.

"'Quality for All': Irmscher's Presidential Speech in Denver." Presidential address. NCTE Convention. Denver, 18 Nov. 1983. Excerpted by Jane Christensen and Diane Allen. *College English* 46 (1984): 143–44; *English Journal* 73.2 (1984): 111–12; *Language Arts* 61 (1984): 204–5.

"An Interview with William F. Irmscher." *The Writing Instructor* 4 (1984): 7–12.

Works Cited

Notes on Contributors

Works Cited

Abbreviations

CE	*College English*
CCC	*College Composition and Communication*
CCCC	Conference on College Composition and Communication
NCTE	National Council of Teachers of English
RR	*Rhetoric Review*
RTE	*Research in the Teaching of English*
WPA	*WPA: Writing Program Administration*

Anderson, Chris. "The Very Style of Faith: Frederick Buechner as Homilist and Essayist." *Christianity and Literature* 38.2 (1989): 7–21.

Annas, Pamela J. "Style as Politics: A Feminist Approach to the Teaching of Writing." *CE* 47 (1985): 360–71.

Anson, Chris, ed. *Writing and Response: Theory, Practice, and Research.* Urbana, IL: NCTE, 1989.

Aristotle. *Rhetoric.* Trans. W. Rhys Roberts. *The Basic Works of Aristotle.* Ed. Richard McKeon. New York: Random, 1941. 1318–1451.

Austin, J. L. *How to Do Things with Words.* Cambridge: Harvard UP, 1962.

Bakhtin, Mikhail. *The Dialogic Imagination.* Trans. Caryl Emerson and Michael Holquist. Ed. Michael Holquist. Austin: U of Texas P, 1981.

———. *Problems of Dostoyevsky's Poetics.* Trans. and ed. Caryl Emerson. Theory and History of Literature 8. Minneapolis: U of Minnesota P, 1984.

————. *Speech Genres and Other Late Essays.* Trans. Vern W. McGee. Ed. Caryl Emerson and Michael Holquist. Austin: U of Texas P, 1986.

Barth, Karl. *The Word of God and the Word of Man.* Trans. Douglas Horton. New York: Harper, 1957.

Bartholomae, David. "Inventing the University." *Journal of Basic Writing* 5.1 (1986): 4–23.

————. "The Study of Error." *CCC* 31 (1980): 253–69.

Belenky, Mary Field, et al. *Women's Ways of Knowing: The Development of Self, Voice, and Mind.* New York: Basic, 1986.

Berlin, James. "Contemporary Composition: The Major Pedagogical Theories." *CE* 44 (1982): 765–77.

————. "Rhetoric and Ideology in the Writing Class." *CE* 50 (1988): 477–94.

————. *Rhetoric and Reality: Writing Instruction in American Colleges, 1900–1985.* Carbondale: Southern Illinois UP, 1987.

Berthoff, Ann E. "From Problem Solving to a Theory of Imagination." *CE* 33 (1972): 636–49.

————. *The Making of Meaning: Metaphors, Models, and Maxims for Writing Teachers.* Montclair, NJ: Boynton, 1981.

Bissex, Glenda L. "What Is a Teacher-Researcher?" Bissex and Bullock 3–5.

Bissex, Glenda L., and Richard H. Bullock, eds. *Seeing for Ourselves: Case-Study Research by Teachers of Writing.* Portsmouth, NH: Heinemann, 1987.

Blair, Catherine Pastore. "Only One of the Voices: Dialogic Writing Across the Curriculum." *CE* 50 (1988): 383–89.

Bledstein, Burton J. *The Culture of Professionalism: The Middle Class and the Development of Higher Education in America.* New York: Norton, 1976.

Booth, Wayne C. "Freedom of Interpretation: Bakhtin and the Challenge of Feminist Criticism." *Bakhtin: Essays and Dialogues on His Work.* Ed. Gary Saul Morson. Chicago: U of Chicago P, 1981. 145–76.

Boulding, Kenneth E. *A Primer on Social Dynamics: History as Dialectics and Development.* New York: Free Press, 1970.

Britton, James. *Language and Learning.* London: Penguin, 1970.

————. "A Quiet Form of Research." Goswami and Stillman 13–19.

Bruffee, Kenneth. "Collaborative Learning and the 'Conversation of Mankind.'" *CE* 46 (1984): 635–52.

Bruner, Jerome. *Actual Minds, Possible Worlds.* Cambridge: Harvard UP, 1986.

Buechner, Frederick. *The Alphabet of Grace.* New York: Harper, 1970.

————. *Now and Then.* New York: Harper, 1983.

————. *The Sacred Journey.* New York: Harper, 1982.

Bullock, Richard H. "When Administration Becomes Scholarship: The Future of Writing Program Administration." *WPA* 11.1–2 (1987): 13–18.

Burke, Kenneth. *A Grammar of Motives*. Berkeley: U of California P, 1969.

———. *A Rhetoric of Motives*. Berkeley: U of California P, 1969.

———. *A Rhetoric of Religion*. Boston: Beacon, 1961.

Callahan, Raymond E. *Education and the Cult of Efficiency*. Chicago: U of Chicago P, 1962.

Campbell, Oscar James. *The Teaching of College English*. NCTE English Monograph 3. New York: Appleton, 1934.

Chase, Geoffrey. "Accommodation, Resistance and the Politics of Student Writing." *CCC* 39 (1988): 13–22.

Cole, Peter, and J. L. Morgan, eds. *Syntax and Semantics 3: Speech Acts*. New York: Academic, 1975.

Coles, William E., Jr., and James Vopat. *What Makes Writing Good: A Multiperspective*. Lexington, MA: Heath, 1985.

Combies, Patricia. "The Struggle to Establish a Profession: An Historical Survey of the Status of College Composition Teachers, 1900–1950." Diss. Carnegie Mellon U, 1987.

Conference on College Composition and Communication. *Statement of Principles and Standards for the Postsecondary Teaching of Writing*. Urbana, IL: NCTE, 1989.

Cooper, Marilyn M. "Context as Vehicle: Implicatures in Writing." Nystrand, *What Writers Know* 105–28.

Coppersmith, Syd, and John R. Garrow. "Results of Student Attitude Survey." Close-out Report to the Buhl Foundation, Writing Across the Business Disciplines, Robert Morris College, Pittsburgh, PA, 31 March 1986.

Coulthard, Malcolm. *An Introduction to Discourse Analysis*. New ed. London: Longman, 1985.

Dasenbrock, Reed Way. "J. L. Austin and the Articulation of a New Rhetoric." *CCC* 38 (1987): 291–305.

Dean, Terry. "Multicultural Classrooms, Monocultural Teachers." *CCC* 40 (1989): 23–37.

Dias, Patrick. "Becoming Students to Learn about Teaching." *English Education* 21 (1989): 196–208.

Didion, Joan. "Why I Write." *New York Times* 5 Dec. 1976, sec. 7: 2.

Diederich, Paul B. *Measuring Growth in English*. Urbana, IL: NCTE, 1974.

Dillard, Annie. "Seeing." *Pilgrim at Tinker Creek*. New York: Harper's Magazine P, 1974. 14–34.

———. "Singing with the Fundamentalists." *Yale Review* 74 (1985): 312–20. Rpt. in *In-Depth: Essayists for Our Time*. Ed. Carl Klaus, Chris Anderson, and Rebecca Faery. New York: Harcourt, 1989. 194–202.

Dillon, George L. *Constructing Texts: Elements of a Theory of Composition and Style*. Bloomington: Indiana UP, 1981.

Dowst, Kenneth. "The Epistemic Approach: Writing, Knowing, and Learning." *Eight Approaches to Teaching Composition*. Ed. Timothy R. Donovan and Ben W. McClelland. Urbana, IL: NCTE, 1980. 65–85.

Edgar, Henry C. *A Minimum Course in Rhetoric.* New York: Appleton, 1922.

Elbow, Peter, and Pat Belanoff. *A Community of Writers: A Workshop Course in Writing.* New York: Random, 1989.

———. *Sharing and Responding.* New York: Random, 1989.

Eliot, Charles. "Wherein Popular Education Has Failed." *The Forum* 14 (1892): 411–28.

Emerson, Ralph Waldo. *Selections from Ralph Waldo Emerson.* Ed. Stephen E. Whicher. Boston: Houghton, 1960.

Epstein, Daniel Mark. "The Case of Harry Houdini." *The Best American Essays 1987.* Ed. Gay Talese. New York: Ticknor and Fields, 1987. 70–84.

Faigley, Lester. "Competing Theories of Process: A Critique and a Proposal." *CE* 48 (1986): 527–42.

Farris, Christine. "Constructing a Theory of Composition: An Ethnographic Study of Four New Teaching Assistants in English." Diss. U. of Washington, 1987.

Flower, Linda. "Writer-Based Prose: A Cognitive Basis for Problems in Writing." *CE* 41 (1979): 19–37.

Flower, Linda, and John R. Hayes. "A Cognitive Process Theory of Writing." *CCC* 32 (1981): 365–87.

Fowler, Roger, ed. *A Dictionary of Modern Critical Terms.* London: Routledge, 1987.

Freedman, Sarah Warshauer. *Response to Student Writing.* Urbana, IL: NCTE, 1987.

Fulwiler, Toby. "How Well Does Writing Across the Curriculum Work?" *CE* 46 (1984): 113–25.

Fulwiler, Toby, and Art Young, eds. *Language Connections: Writing and Reading Across the Curriculum.* Urbana, IL: NCTE, 1982.

Gadamer, Hans-Georg. *Reason in the Age of Science.* Trans. Frederick G. Lawrence. Cambridge: MIT P, 1986.

Geertz, Clifford. *The Interpretation of Cultures.* New York: Basic, 1973.

Gibson, Walker. *Tough, Sweet, and Stuffy: An Essay on Modern American Styles.* Bloomington: Indiana UP, 1966.

Giroux, Henry A. *Theory and Resistance in Education.* South Hadley, MA: Bergin and Garvey, 1983.

Giroux, Henry A., and Peter McLaren. "Teacher Education and the Politics of Engagement: A Case for Democratic Schooling." *Harvard Educational Review* 56 (1986): 213–38.

Glick, Milton D. "Writing Across the Curriculum: A Dean's Perspective." *WPA* 11.3 (1988): 53–58.

Goswami, Dixie, and Peter R. Stillman, eds. *Reclaiming the Classroom.* Upper Montclair, NJ: Boynton, 1987.

Graff, Gerald. *Professing Literature: An Institutional History.* Chicago: U of Chicago P, 1987.

Grice, H. Paul. "Logic and Conversation." Cole and Morgan 41–58.

Griffin, C. W. "Programs for Writing Across the Curriculum: A Report." *CCC* 36 (1985): 398–403.

Gumperz, John J., and Dell Hymes. *Directions in Sociolinguistics: The Ethnography of Communication.* New York: Holt, 1972.

Hadden, Jeffrey, and Charles E. Swann. *Prime Time Preachers: The Rising Power of Televangelism.* Reading, MA: Addison-Wesley, 1981.

Hairston, Maxine. "Some Speculations about the Future of Writing Programs." *WPA* 11.3 (1988): 9–16.

Halliday, M.A.K., and Ruqaiya Hasan. *Cohesion in English.* London: Longman, 1976.

Harris, Jeanette, and Christine Hult. "Using a Survey of Writing Assignments to Make Informed Curricular Decisions." *WPA* 8.3 (1985): 7–14.

Harris, Joseph. "The Idea of Community in the Study of Writing." *CCC* 40 (1989): 11–22.

Harste, Jerome C., Virginia A. Woodward, and Carolyn L. Burke. "Examining Our Assumptions: A Transactional View of Literacy and Learning." *RTE* 18 (1984): 84–108.

Heath, Shirley Brice. *Ways with Words: Language, Life, and Work in Communities and Classrooms.* New York: Cambridge UP, 1983.

Heller, Scott. "Fifty Lecturers Lose Their Jobs in a Dispute over How—and If—Writing Can Be Taught." *Chronicle of Higher Education* 17 April 1985: 23–24.

Hillocks, George, Jr. *Research on Written Composition: New Directions for Teaching.* Urbana, IL: ERIC/NCTE, 1986.

Hirsch, E. D., Jr. *Cultural Literacy.* New York: Random-Vintage, 1988.

Horvath, Brooke K. "The Components of Written Response: A Practical Synthesis of Current Views." *RR* 2 (1984): 136–56.

Hymes, Dell. *Foundations in Sociolinguistics: An Ethnographic Approach.* Philadelphia: U of Pennsylvania P, 1974.

Irmscher, William F. *Teaching Expository Writing.* New York: Holt, 1979.

Johnson, Burges, and Helene Hartley. *Written Composition in America.* Union, NJ: Union College, 1936.

Kalmbach, James R. "The Politics of Research." Young and Fulwiler 217–27.

Kelly, George. *A Theory of Personality: The Psychology of Personal Constructs.* New York: Norton, 1963.

Kingston, Maxine Hong. *The Woman Warrior.* New York: Random-Vintage, 1977.

Kinneavy, James. *The Greek Rhetorical Roots of Early Christian Faith.* New York: Oxford, 1987.

———. "Writing Across the Curriculum." *ADE Bulletin* 76 (1983): 14–21.

——— "Writing Across the Curriculum." *Teaching Composition: Twelve Bib-

liographical Essays. Ed. Gary Tate. Fort Worth: Texas Christian UP, 1987. 353–77.

Kirsch, Gesa. "Writing Across the Curriculum: The Program at Third College, University of California, San Diego." *WPA* 12.1–2 (1988): 47–55.

Knoblauch, C. H. "Rhetorical Constructions: Dialogue and Commitment." *CE* 50 (1988): 125–40.

Knoblauch, C. H., and Lil Brannon. *Rhetorical Traditions and the Teaching of Writing.* Montclair, NJ: Boynton, 1984.

Kroll, Barry M., and John C. Shafer. "Error Analysis and the Teaching of Composition." *CCC* 29 (1978): 242–48.

Labov, William, and David Fanshel. *Therapeutic Discourse: Psychotherapy as Conversation.* New York: Academic, 1977.

Larson, Magali Sarfatti. *The Rise of Professionalism: A Sociological Analysis.* Berkeley: U of California P, 1977.

LeFevre, Karen Burke. *Invention as a Social Act.* Carbondale: Southern Illinois UP, 1987.

Levinson, Stephen C. *Pragmatics.* Cambridge: Cambridge UP, 1983.

Lloyd-Jones, Richard. "Primary Trait Scoring." *Evaluating Writing: Describing, Measuring, Judging.* Ed. Charles R. Cooper and Lee Odell. Urbana, IL: NCTE, 1977. 33–66.

Lunsford, Ronald F. "Teaching the Writing Process: A Case Study of First-Year Teaching Assistants." CCCC Convention. Minneapolis, 21 March 1985.

Lunsford, Ronald F., and Richard Straub. *Twelve Readers Reading.* New York: Random. Forthcoming.

McCleod, Susan. "Defining Writing Across the Curriculum." *WPA* 11.1–2 (1987): 19–24.

McCord, Phyllis Frus. "Reading Nonfiction in Composition Courses: From Theory to Practice." *CE* 47 (1985): 747–62.

McCormick, Kathleen, Gary Waller, and Linda Flower. *Reading Texts: Reading, Responding, Writing.* Lexington, MA: Heath, 1987.

McLuhan, Marshall. *Understanding Media: The Extensions of Man.* New York: McGraw-Hill, 1964.

Martin, Nancy. "On the Move: Teacher-Researchers." Goswami and Stillman 20–28.

Miller, James E., Jr. *Word, Self, Reality: The Rhetoric of Imagination.* New York: Dodd, 1972.

Mohr, Marion M., and Marion S. Maclean. *Working Together: A Guide for Teacher-Researchers.* Urbana, IL: NCTE, 1987.

Murray, Donald M. *Write to Learn.* New York: Holt, 1984.

Nystrand, Martin. "Reciprocity as a Principle of Discourse." *The Structure of Written Communication: Studies of Reciprocity Between Writers and Readers.* Orlando: Academic, 1986. 39–58.

————. "Rhetoric's 'Audience' and Linguistics' 'Speech Community': Implications for Understanding Writing, Reading, and Text." Nystrand, *What Writers Know* 1–28.

————. "A Social-Interactive Model of Writing." *Written Communication* 6 (1989): 66–85.

————, ed. *What Writers Know: The Language, Process, and Structure of Written Discourse.* New York: Academic, 1982.

Nystrand, Martin, and Deborah Brandt. "Response to Writing as a Context for Learning to Write." Anson 209–30.

Nystrand, Martin, Anne Doyle, and Margaret Himley. "A Critical Examination of the Doctrine of Autonomous Texts." *The Structure of Written Communication: Studies of Reciprocity Between Writers and Readers.* Orlando: Academic, 1986. 81–107.

Olney, James. *Metaphors of the Self: The Meaning of Autobiography.* Princeton: Princeton UP, 1972.

Olson, David R. "From Utterance to Text: The Bias of Language in Speech and Writing." *Harvard Educational Review* 47 (1977): 257–81.

Olson, Gary A., and Joseph M. Moxley. "Directing Freshman Composition: The Limits of Authority." *CCC* 40 (1989): 51–60.

Parker, Robert P. "Writing Courses for Teachers: From Practice to Theory." *CCC* 32 (1982): 411–19.

Percy, Walker. *The Message in the Bottle.* 1954. New York: Farrar, 1979.

Perelman, Les. "The Context of Classroom Writing." *CE* 48 (1986): 471–79.

Petersen, Bruce T., ed. *Convergences: Transactions in Reading and Writing.* Urbana, IL: NCTE, 1986.

Petrosky, Anthony R. "From Story to Essay: Reading and Writing." *CCC* 33 (1982): 19–36.

Podis, Leonard A., and Joanne M. Podis. "Improving Our Responses to Student Writing: A Process-Oriented Approach." *RR* 5 (1986): 90–98.

Polanyi, Michael. *Personal Knowledge: Towards a Post-Critical Philosophy.* Chicago: U of Chicago P, 1962.

Postman, Neil. *Amusing Ourselves to Death: Public Discourse in the Age of Show Business.* New York: Penguin, 1985.

Probst, Robert E. "Transactional Theory and Response to Student Writing." Anson 68–79.

Purves, Alan C. "The Teacher as Reader: An Anatomy." *CE* 46 (1984): 259–65.

Reddy, Michael J. "The Conduit Metaphor: A Case of Frame Conflict in Our Language about Language." *Metaphor and Thought.* Ed. Andrew Ortony. Cambridge: Cambridge UP, 1979. 284–324.

Richards, I. A. *The Philosophy of Rhetoric.* New York: Oxford UP, 1936.

Rommetveit, Ragmar. *On Message Structure: A Framework for the Study of Language and Communication.* London: Wiley, 1974.

Rorty, Richard. *Philosophy and the Mirror of Nature.* Princeton: Princeton UP, 1979.

Rosenblatt, Louise M. *The Reader, the Text, the Poem: The Transactional Theory of the Literary Work.* Carbondale: Southern Illinois UP, 1978.

Rudolph, Frederick. *Curriculum: A History of the American Undergraduate Course of Study since 1636.* San Franciso: Jossey-Bass, 1978.

Russell, David R. "Romantics on Writing: Liberal Culture and the Abolition of Composition Courses." *RR* 6 (1988): 132–48.

———. "Writing Across the Curriculum and the Communications Movement: Some Lessons from the Past." *CCC* 38 (1987): 184–94.

Schenkein, J., ed. *Studies in the Organization of Conversational Interaction.* New York: Academic, 1978.

Schon, Donald A. *The Reflective Practitioner: How Professionals Think in Action.* New York: Basic, 1983.

Schuster, Charles. "The Power of Play." *The Clearinghouse* 60 (1987): 296–99.

———. "Situational Sequencing." *The Writing Instructor* 3 (1984): 177–84.

Schwartz, Mimi. "Wearing the Shoe on the Other Foot: Teacher as Student Writer." *CCC* 40 (1989): 203–10.

Searle, John R. "Indirect Speech Acts." Cole and Morgan 59–82.

———. *Speech Acts.* Cambridge: Cambridge UP, 1969.

Shaughnessy, Mina P. *Errors and Expectations: A Guide for the Teacher of Basic Writing.* New York: Oxford UP, 1977.

Shelly, Lynn Buncher. "The Writer and the Text: Deconstruction and the Teaching of Composition." Diss. U of Pittsburgh, 1984.

Shipherd, H. Robinson. *Manual and Models for College Composition.* Boston: Ginn, 1928.

Shor, Ira. *Critical Teaching and Everyday Life.* Chicago: U of Chicago P, 1987.

Sipple, Jo-Ann M. "A Planning Process for Building Writing-Across-the-Curriculum Programs to Last." *Journal of Higher Education.* Forthcoming.

Sipple, Jo-Ann M., and Chris D. Stenberg. "Writing in Business and Other Disciplines at Robert Morris College." *The Writing Across the Curriculum Book.* Ed. Toby Fulwiler and Art Young. Portsmouth, NH: Boynton. Forthcoming.

Smith, Frank. "A Metaphor for Literacy: Creating Worlds or Shunting Information?" *Literacy, Language, and Learning: The Nature and Consequences of Reading and Writing.* Ed. David R. Olson, Nancy Torrance, and Angela Hildyard. Cambridge: Cambridge UP, 1985. 195–213.

Smith, Louise Z. "Why English Departments Should 'House' Writing Across the Curriculum." *CE* 50 (1988): 390–95.

Sommers, Nancy. "Narrative as Convention, Culture, and Ideology." CCCC Convention. St. Louis, 17 March 1988.

———. "Responding to Student Writing." *CCC* (1982): 148–56.

Steinmann, Martin, Jr. "Speech Act Theory and Writing." Nystrand, *What Writers Know* 291–323.

Stewart, Donald. "Some Facts Worth Knowing about the Origins of Freshman Composition." *CEA Critic* 44 (1982): 2–11.

Swanson-Owens, Deborah. "Identifying Natural Sources of Resistance: A Case Study of Implementing Writing Across the Curriculum." *RTE* 20 (1986): 69–97.

Tannen, Deborah. *Coherence in Spoken and Written Discourse.* Norwood, NJ: Ablex, 1984.

———, ed. *Spoken and Written Language: Exploring Orality and Literacy.* Norwood, NJ: Ablex, 1982.

Trimbur, John. "Collaborative Learning and Teaching Writing." *Perspectives on Research and Scholarship in Composition.* Ed. Ben W. McClelland and Timothy R. Donovan. New York: MLA, 1985. 87–109.

———. "Cultural Studies and Teaching Writing." *Focuses* 1 (1988): 5–18.

Veysey, Laurence R. *The Emergence of the American University.* Chicago: U of Chicago P, 1965.

Voloshinov, V. N. "Discourse in Life and Discourse in Art." Appendix 1. *Freudianism: A Critical Sketch.* Trans. I. R. Titunik. Ed. I. R. Titunik and Neal Bruss. 1976. Bloomington: Indiana UP, 1987.

Weaver, Constance. "Parallels Between New Paradigms in Science and in Reading and Literary Theories: An Essay Review." *RTE* 19 (1985): 298–316.

White, Edward M. "Post-Structural Literary Criticism and the Response to Student Writing." *CCC* 35 (1984): 186–95.

Williams, Joseph. "The Phenomenology of Error." *CCC* 32 (1981): 152–68.

Williams, Raymond. *Marxism and Literature.* New York: Oxford UP, 1977.

Young, Art, and Toby Fulwiler, eds. *Writing Across the Disciplines: Research into Practice.* Upper Montclair, NJ: Boynton, 1986.

Young, Richard E., Alton L. Becker, and Kenneth L. Pike. *Rhetoric: Discovery and Change.* New York: Harcourt, 1970.

Notes on Contributors

CHRIS ANDERSON is Associate Professor of English and Composition Coordinator at Oregon State University, author of *Style as Argument* (Southern Illinois University Press, 1987), and editor of *Literary Nonfiction* (Southern Illinois, 1989) and *The Tyrannies of Virtue* (University of Oklahoma Press, 1990). His Ph.D. is from the University of Washington, where Bill Irmscher salvaged not only his dissertation but his self-esteem.

MARY LOUISE BULEY-MEISSNER is Assistant Professor of English at the University of Wisconsin–Milwaukee. In the late 1970s and the early 1980s she worked as Bill Irmscher's assistant in the Freshman Composition Program at the University of Washington. She also wrote her dissertation under his supervision, a project they continued by mail when she left to teach in China. Without his patience and encouragement, she still might be in Yangzhou writing chapter 12.

VIRGINIA A. CHAPPELL is Assistant Professor of English at Marquette University. She completed her doctoral dissertation under Bill Irmscher's direction in 1988 at the University of Washington. As a graduate student and a staff member of that university's Educational Opportunity Program Writing Center, she spent many hours in Bill's office discussing students and policies and how many more of her carefully wrought sentences would have to be split in two to satisfy his exacting editorial eye.

EDWARD P. J. CORBETT is Professor of English at Ohio State University. He has known Bill Irmscher since serving as a member of the CCCC Executive Committee in 1965, and he succeeded Bill as the editor of *CCC* (1974–79). He is the author of *Classical Rhetoric for the Modern Student* (Oxford University Press, 3d ed., 1990) and *The Little English Handbook* (Scott, Foresman, 5th ed., 1987).

KATHLEEN DOTY is Assistant Professor of English at Humboldt State University, Arcata, California, where she teaches linguistics and literature. She received her Ph.D. from the University of Washington, where Bill Irmscher once said to her, "But isn't pragmatics simply rhetoric?" His question prompted the essay included here.

CHRISTINE R. FARRIS is Assistant Professor of English and Research Coordinator for the Campus-Wide Writing Center at Indiana University–Bloomington. Her Ph.D. is from the University of Washington, where Bill Irmscher directed her dissertation. She hopes that Irmscher's advice to the group of new TAs of which she was a member will continue to guide her dealings with students and colleagues as it guided Irmscher's: "In matters of writing, we must forgive each other much."

ANNE RUGGLES GERE is Professor of English and Professor of Education at the University of Michigan, where she serves as codirector of the Ph.D. program in English education. From 1975 to 1987 she was a colleague of Bill Irmscher at the University of Washington. Her recent publications include *Writing Groups* (Southern Illinois University Press, 1987) and *The Active Reader* (Holt, 1990).

RICHARD LLOYD-JONES is Professor of English at the University of Iowa, where he received his Ph.D. in 1956. In 1986 he stepped down as department chair but continues overseeing Iowa's Programs in Letters. As past chair of CCCC, past president of NCTE, and a former member of both the NCTE editorial board and the Commission on Composition, he has frequently worked with Bill Irmscher over the years.

CHARLES I. SCHUSTER is Director of Composition and Coordinator of the Graduate Rhetoric and Composition Program at the University of Wisconsin–Milwaukee. He came to know Bill Irmscher as a colleague when he began his career as Assistant Professor of English at the University of Washington. Professor Schuster didn't learn much from Bill, only little things like how to direct a writing program, how to create positive relations between faculty and graduate students, how to live in a department, live in a profession, write and think clearly and cogently, maintain high standards—just the little things.

KURT SPELLMEYER is Assistant Professor of English and Director of the Writing Program at Rutgers University in New Brunswick, New Jersey. He began teaching composition under Bill Irmscher at the University of

Washington, and it was Irmscher's work on Burke which first awakened him to the cultural and political dimensions of language instruction.

RICHARD TRACEY is Director of Writing Programs for Jostens Learning Corporation, for which he supervises the development of K–12 word processing tools, electronic mail systems, and writing process courseware; he also conducts workshops for school clients across North America on the theory and practice of rhetoric and composition. In 1981 Bill Irmscher selected Tracey for his NEH Summer Seminar for College Teachers. With Bill's encouragement he then entered the graduate program at Washington, where, as Bill's last doctoral student, he earned his Ph.D. in 1989.

RICHARD YOUNG is Professor of Rhetoric and English Literature at Carnegie Mellon and Director of the Language Across the Curriculum Program. Previously he was Head of the Department of English at Carnegie Mellon, where he oversaw the development of its graduate programs in rhetoric. He has known Bill Irmscher forever, or at least since 1964, when as editor of *CCC* Bill had the good sense to turn down a badly written article on audience analysis which has never yet seen the light of day.